The White Cat

A pantomime

Norman Robbins

Samuel French — London
New York - Toronto - Hollywood

ISBN 0 573 16425 8

Please see page iv for further copyright information

CHARACTERS

Mother Goose, an Immortal
Ghiselle, her pet Goose
Ambrose, the Court Chamberlain
King Pat-a-cake, Ruler of Euphoria
Venoma, the Witch-Queen of Despondia
Dame Hernia Lovelorn, Nurse and Guardian to
   Rosamund
Princess Rosamund, Heir to The Seven Kingdoms
Peter Piper, a Groom in the King's stables
Prince Fyne, the King's eldest son
Prince Dandi, his second son
Prince Peerless, his youngest son
Bluemalkin, the White Cat's servant
Esmeralda, a Gypsy leader
Peglegasus, a Royal Horse
Tigger-toes, a very Jazzy Cat (dancer only)

Chorus of Citizens, Courtiers, Servants, Cats, etc.

SYNOPSIS OF SCENES

ACT I

INTERVAL

ACT II

AUTHOR'S NOTES

Like *King of the Golden Mountain, A Frog He Would a Wooing Go, King Hummingtop* and dozens of other Victorian pantomimes, *The White Cat* vanished from the pantomime roster almost a hundred years ago. Its last production was, I believe, at the Drury Lane theatre in 1904, (that particular version being written by J. Hickory Wood and Arthur Collins) but for many years prior to this, it was a very popular subject.

Based on a story by the French Countess d'Aulnois, it was first seen in 1811 at the Lyceum Theatre as *The White Cat; or Harlequin in Fairy Wood*, though typically of the pantomimes of that period, the story part served only to set the comical Harlequinade in motion. In 1842, however, at Covent Garden theatre it was presented as a fairy *extravaganza* (written by that brilliant man of the theatre, J. R. Planche) as a vehicle for the sensational Lucy Vestris, to whom the theatre world owes so much. Following its huge success in this form, its innovations were quickly adapted by other managements for pantomime use and continued to delight audiences for the next 60 years until mysteriously it fell from favour.

Whilst researching *Slapstick and Sausages*, my book on pantomime's evolution, I was kindly and unexpectedly loaned original copies of the Planche *extravaganza* and the Hickory Wood/Collins version of *The White Cat*, both of which I read with interest. The latter was a world away from Planche's beautifully rhymed and touching couplets, its comic fairy making "her" first entrance on a wire, and many zany characters being introduced to carry the story forward. There was even a short Harlequinade (from which modern pantomimes developed) tagged on to the end of it and (unusually for pantomimes of any era) three acts. Both, however, must have been spectacular to watch, and again made me wonder how the story could have been ignored for so long.

Having a strong dislike for comic fairies, it took me some time to formulate my own pantomime version of the story and adapt it for amateur usage, but eventually the scenes took shape and modern technology has enabled me to include one section that would have been impossible for Victorian audiences to see, but would have delighted the Countess d'Aulnois who described it so beautifully in her original story; the ghostly hands. In offering this version of *The White Cat*, I'm assuming that today's audiences will be as enthralled by this unusual story as I was. The potential for an experienced production company is awesome, yet even the smallest pantomime society should find it within their capabilities. For those with limited resources I include a few production hints overleaf.

Norman Robbins

PRODUCTION NOTES

White Cat and Bluemalkin would appear at first glance to be problem characters. They are, however, no more of a problem than Puss in *Puss in Boots*, and are in fact, much simpler to costume because only the heads and hands are ever seen. White Cat's headpiece is of white fur material (which can be purchased fairly cheaply at almost any material shop), close fitting to the head, full face opening, and fastened under the chin. It should be long enough at the bottom to be tucked well into the high neckline of the dress. A moulded cat mask covers most of the face, but the mouth should be free for speech. Bluemalkin's headpiece is exactly the same, but blue-grey in colouring and she also wears a mask. (Most carnival or fancy dress shops stock these and if only full face ones are available, they can be cut with scissors to the required dimensions.) Both wear mittens of matching fur to their heads and their tails are also made of the same material. The dresses of both are floor length, loose fitting, high-necked and long-sleeved. White Cat is dressed in cream, white or ivory, Bluemalkin in whatever appears suitable, but the same style. The White Cat's costume could be decorated with diamonté or silver sequins, as the more splendid she looks the better.

The White Cat's great hooded cloak should be all-enveloping and trimmed with white fur. Nothing but the half mask should be seen of her when she appears at the Court. After her distressed exit a body double should put on the cloak and mask for the second entrance. When the Black-out comes, the body double exits and is replaced by the Princess. If there is any problem with this, the girl playing the White Cat/Princess role must turn upstage after the dagger incident, and everyone cluster round her as she discards the cloak and mask in the Black-out. The Princess costume, of course, would be worn underneath the cloak. When the lights return, everyone falls back to reveal the Princess. The first option, however, is a better effect.

The Cat Chorus and/or Dancers wear the same kind of headpieces and mittens as above, and although described as being in Court dress, could, if preferred, be in tights and body stockings, plus furry mittens and tails.

Tigger-toes should be outstandingly coloured as a solo dancer or singer.

For the UV or Black Light sequence, only four people are needed to work this. They should be totally clothed in black, including faces, (black net over the eyes) and wear pure white gloves. The table should be totally black and therefore invisible. The tablecloth has a black backing which faces the audience, white side upstage. When the black side is lowered on to the table, the white side suddenly becomes visible to the watcher. Chair, salvers, salver covers, foods, plates and cutlery, etc., are all painted on to hardboard in UV paint. (Artists' stores should be able to get these easily and many colours are available.) Salver covers are separate to the dish holding the food and are simply held in front of the food. Lifting the obstructing cover causes the food to miraculously appear. Prince Peerless's Act II costume should also be made of UV materials or edged in UV material or paint. This effect does need a lot of rehearsal to get a polished result, as experienced societies know, but it's well worth the effort.

If for some reason your society is unable to do a UV scene, the script is written in such a way that it can easily be omitted. On the Prince's entrance to the enchanted Palace, just lower the lights, allow the White Cat to get into position, then take the lights back to normal.

For the "Tree of Truth" routine, it is suggested that tennis balls or similar, painted orange, are used for the oranges. They're just about the right size and not too hard on the skull when dropped from a height. Polystyrene balls are also useful and can be made out of old packing material and shaped with a soft-wire suede brush. It's a messy job, with bits flying all over the place, but it's cheap and can take water based paint very well. You do need about fifty, though. If other fruits are used, just alter the lines. The gag remains the same and after a hundred years, still brings the place down.

for

GRAHAM AND AVRIL CHAMBERS

of Gloucester, Canada.

"Just a small token…"

ACT I

Mother Goose's Arbour

A frontcloth scene depicting a gigantic shimmering spider's web suspended between huge dew-spangled roses

The Lighting should suggest early morning and, if possible, a light mist should be visible

When the main CURTAIN *rises to reveal this, Mother Goose is standing* DC, *a beaming smile on her face. She is everyone's idea of a friendly grandmother and dressed in the traditional garb of the nursery-rhyme character, carries a large wooden spoon which she uses as a wand. Beside her is Ghiselle, her pet goose*

Mother Goose (*brightly*) Hallo, my dears, and welcome to my Arbour of
  Delight.
  I'm Mother Goose, your friend and guide throughout the show
  tonight. (*She drops a curtsy*)
  (*Wryly*) At least, that's my intention, though I'm very sad to
  say,
  Some modern critics now declare that panto should be swept
  away,
  Because, although for years on earth
  You've marvelled at the tales I've told,
  In these dot.com and e-mail times,
  They're simply too well known and *old*.
  (*With determination*) Well…
  Tonight there'll *be* no Pumpkin Coach;
  No Magic Lamp or Cave.
  No Beanstalks; Babes; or London Bells, or
  Ship-wrecked sailors we must save.
  We'll do without a Giant and ignore old Humpty's fall;
  I'll tell *instead* a tale that's barely known today at all.
  And ere this ev'ning's over, trust you'll find you're happy that

You came to hear the story of the fabulous White Cat.
(*Brightly*) So no prevarication. I'll whisk you all away
To where, as in *all* fairy tales, imagination still holds sway.
This time it's old Euphoria, for in that Kingdom fair
Its people wait to greet you—in the ancient City Square.

Mother Goose brandishes her spoon and exits R, followed by Ghiselle as the Lights rapidly fade to a Black-out and the backdrop flies out

SCENE 1

The Kingdom of Euphoria

The Lights come up at once to reveal an ancient city square with stylized buildings and cobbled streets in the background. Other buildings hide entrances and exits L and R. Suggested period, 14th Century

When the scene begins, it is a bright, sunny day and the Citizens of Euphoria are singing and dancing

No. 1 Song (Citizens)

At the end of the routine they fall back into small groups, silently chatting and laughing

Ambrose, the elderly Court Chamberlain, hurries in UC and moves DC, looking very anxious and glancing around hastily

Ambrose (*dismayed*) Oh, my goodness. Look at the poor things. Laughing and joking as though they haven't a care in the world.
Citizens (*brightly*) Good morning, Lord Chamberlain.
Ambrose (*flustered*) Never mind "Good morning". Everyone hide. Quick. Quick. We're in terrible danger. (*He attempts to shoo them away*)
Citizen 1 (*stepping forward*) But why? What's happened?
Ambrose (*agitated*) It's Queen *Venoma*. She's heading this way and she's probably got her horrible son, Prince Ghastly with her. Run. Run. (*He shoos them again*)

No-one moves

Citizen 2 (*puzzled*) Queen Venoma? Prince Ghastly? Who on earth are *they*?

Everyone shrugs and shakes their head

Ambrose (*horrified*) Don't you *know*? (*Faintly*) Oh, my goodness. I don't believe it. We thought *everyone* knew about *them*. (*He gathers himself*) She's the world's wickedest witch, and *he's* its most ugly man.

Citizens react

Citizen 3 (*worried*) But what do they want in Euphoria?

Ambrose (*helplessly*) Who knows? But whatever it is, they'll get it. They always do. (*Mournfully*) And they'll be here at any minute.

Citizen 4 In that case we better *had* be off. And we won't come back till they've gone again. (*To others*) Come on, everyone. You can hide in *my* house.

Citizens quickly exit UL, *leaving Ambrose shrouded in gloom. He suddenly realizes and hurries* L

Ambrose (*calling after them*) Wait. Wait. (*Dismayed*) Oh, dear. They've gone. (*To the audience*) I was going to ask if they'd seen King Pat-a-cake today. He left the Palace almost an hour ago and I can't find him *anywhere*. If he's not here when Queen Venoma arrives she'll be *furious*.

There is a fanfare and King Pat-a-cake enters UR. *He is an elderly man, not too bright in intellect, but resplendent in royal robes and wearing his gold crown*

As Ambrose turns to see him, the King moves DC

(*Relieved*) Oh, Your Majesty. Thank goodness you're here. I've been searching everywhere. Where have you *been*?

King Down to [local chemist's shop] for some headache tablets. (*Remembering*) And you'll never guess *what*. I'd just left the shop when the chemist came running after me shouting "Stop. Stop. There's been a terrible *mistake*. Instead of giving you aspirin, I've given you arsenic".

Ambrose reacts

"Does it make any difference?" I asked him, and the poor fellow nearly fainted. "Of *course* it does, Your Majesty", he said. "Arsenic's a deadly poison. You owe me another fifty pence."

Ambrose (*reacting, then recovering*) Yes. Well, never mind that, Sire. I've got the most awful news.

King (*grimacing*) Oh, it's not another crime wave, is it? If we catch any more crooks I don't know where we're going to put them. All the prisons are full and so is the House of Commons.

Ambrose (*hastily*) No, no, Your Majesty. It's Queen *Venoma*. She's coming here today and demands to see you.

King (*startled*) What? But she *can't*. It's impossible. Tell her to go away. If she hears the Royal Announcement we'll *never* get rid of her.

Ambrose Can't you *delay* it, Sire? Wait until after she's gone?

King (*aghast*) Certainly *not*. It's the most important announcement I'll *ever* make and everything's just about ready. The Palace has been cleaned from top to bottom and even the *flagpole's* getting a fresh coat of paint.

Ambrose So I noticed, Sire. The workmen were climbing up it, half an hour ago. (*He frowns*) But why were they carrying tape measures?

King (*beaming*) Ah. That was *my* idea. I told them to find out how tall it was so they'd know *exactly* how much paint it would take to do the job.

Ambrose (*frowning*) But wouldn't it have been easier for them to lay the pole on the ground and *then* measure it?

King (*scornfully*) Don't be silly, Ambrose. They need to know how high it is, not how long. (*Remembering*) But never mind that… What are we going to do about *Venoma*? Remember. Her son's a prince, too, and if one word of what we're doing reaches *her* ears, she'll be casting her nasty little spells left, right and centre and helping *him*. Nobody else will get a look in.

Ambrose (*miserably*) You're right, Sire. Oh, if only you'd had children of your *own*. None of this would be happening.

King I know. I know. (*Plaintively*) But how else can I decide who'll get the throne when I retire? Three adopted sons … all princes … and not a thing to choose between them. It's the fairest way I can think of.

Ambrose I quite agree, Sire. But with Venoma around… (*He shrugs helplessly*)

King (*suddenly*) Wait. What if I make the announcement *now*? Before she arrives. (*Eagerly*) By the time she gets here, the boys will be gone and she won't know a thing about it. (*He looks hopeful*)

Ambrose (*brightening*) It's worth a try, Your Majesty. But you'll have to be quick.

King (*firmly*) Then I shall be. Find Their Highnesses at once and tell them to present themselves *immediately*.

Ambrose gives a deep bow and hurries off DR, *leaving the King alone*

(*Chortling*) Oho. I can't *wait* to see their faces when I tell them what they have to do. And the minute one of them *wins*, I can give up the throne and spend the rest of my life doing what *I* want to do. Collecting Pokemon cards [or any current craze]. (*He continues to ad-lib*)

The Lights fade and a green follow spot picks up the gaunt figure of Queen Venoma as she enters DL, *clutching a jewel-topped cane. She is deathly pale, and dressed in a high-necked black gown with green and red sequinned trim. A matching cape flows behind her. A black crown, heavy with red and green jewels is on her head and her taloned fingers are covered in rings*

Unnoticed by the King, she moves DS, *and arriving beside him, waits for him to notice her. King continues ad-libbing for a few moments before he glances at her, nods politely and continues speaking to the audience until realization dawns and a look of horror appears on his face. Slowly he turns his head to look at her properly and recoils in fear*

(*Recovering and forcing a smile*) Queen Venoma.

Venoma (*coldly*) So *this* is the welcome I receive in Euphoria? No flags. (*She indicates vaguely*) No cheering crowds. No-one to greet me at the palace. (*Thoughtfully*) Is it possible my presence is *unwanted* here? (*She fixes the King with a baleful glare*)

King (*gulping*) Unwanted? (*He chuckles nervously*) No. No. Of course not. Nothing of the kind. We're *delighted* to see you. (*He chuckles uneasily*)

Venoma Indeed? (*She smiles nastily*) Then there's no objection to my remaining here until our business is concluded?

King (*hastily*) No. No. Stay as long as you... (*He realizes*) Business? What business?

Venoma Many years ago—in the Land of the Seven Kingdoms—a certain princess was born. A child of such rare beauty, my own beloved son, Prince Ghastly, vowed that on her eighteenth birthday he would return to the royal palace and claim her hand in marriage. (*Malevolently*) Her foolish parents, however, *defied* his wishes, and placing the baby in the care of a common nursemaid, sent them into hiding. Despite my great powers, no trace of them has ever been found. (*She smiles coldly*) But now ... now ... I believe our search has ended.

King (*wide-eyed*) Really?

Venoma (*silkily*) According to my magic crystal, almost twenty years ago, three small children were brought to this Kingdom for adoption.

King (*happily*) That's true. Yes. I took them all myself.

Venoma And what better place to hide a missing princess than the palace of another king? (*She smiles nastily at him*)

King (*realizing*) Oh, no. No. That isn't what happened.

Venoma (*snapping*) Fool. Dolt. Idiot. Do you think I'd be beaten by your pathetic attempt to hide her from me? (*Grimly*) One of your children is Princess Rosamund and today she shall marry my son.

King (*flustered*) But she *can't*. It's impossible.

Venoma What? (*She glares at him*)

King (*hastily*) I mean you don't *understand*. She *isn't* a princess. She's a *prince*. They're *all* princes. Boys. I haven't got a princess.

Venoma (*stunned*) Boys? All *boys*?

King Prince Fyne, Prince Dandi, and Prince Peerless.

Venoma (*turning away in shock and speaking to herself*) Can my powers have failed me? Have we journeyed in vain? (*She gathers herself*) No. No. I won't believe it. The crystal ball is *never* mistaken. Somewhere in this miserable little kingdom, the girl is hiding and *nothing* shall prevent me from finding her. (*She turns back to the King*) Very well. It appears we must seek elsewhere. (*Grimly and slowly*) But should I find you've misled me... (*Savagely*) Then beware the wrath of Venoma.

With gritted teeth, Venoma sweeps past him and exits DL

The green follow spot vanishes and the Lights return to normal

King (*weakly*) Ohhhh. Thank goodness she'd come to the wrong place. By the time she finds a princess, she'll be miles away from here and we'll never see her again. (*He glances off* L) Yes. There she goes. Out of the city gates and into the forest. (*Happily*) I'd better find Ambrose and tell him to spread the good news.

The King hurries off DR

A beaming Dame Lovelorn enters UL, *carrying a mop and bucket. A woman of indeterminate age, she is garbed in an outrageous outfit suggesting that of a housekeeper, with mob cap, apron, and a necklace of brightly coloured beads. She moves* DC *to speak to the audience*

Dame (*chortling*) Oh, I say. What a bonny looking lot. Everybody happy and smiling. Yes. Especially the lady over there. (*She indicates vaguely, then speaks to her*) I bet *you're* pleased to have a night out on your own, aren't you, dear? (*She chuckles*) Yes. And I'm not surprised. You must be shattered. (*To the audience, confidentially*) Sixteen children she's got. (*She nods*) Five boys and eleven girls. I saw her getting on a bus with them last week, (*to "her"*) didn't I, dear? (*She nods*) Yes. (*To the audience*) The driver took one look and said "Good Heavens, Missis. Are all these yours, or is it a picnic?" "Oh, they're all mine", she said, "but believe me, it's no picnic". (*She chortles then remembers*) But I'd better introduce meself, hadn't I? Lovelorn's the name. Hernia Lovelorn. Toast of the Town and Nursemaid to the Stars. (*She chuckles modestly and preens*) Mind you ... there's not been much nursemaiding going on these past few years. That's why I went down to the Job Centre. To see if I could find something else. (*She pulls a face*) But they're not very helpful, are they? The feller behind the counter said "I'm terribly sorry, Madam, but we only have *one* job on

offer today, and that's for a film company in London who want someone
to rub warm baby oil over Leonardo de Cuppachino's [or other current
idol] body, so it'll glisten when he takes his shirt off'. "Ooooh", I said, "It's
exactly the job I'm looking for. How soon can I start?" "Well", he said,
"I'm not exactly sure, but if I were you, I'd get up to Glasgow as soon as
possible". "Just a minute?" I said, "I thought you told me this job was in
London. Why do I have to go to Glasgow?" "Well", he said, "that's where
the end of the queue is". (*Brightening*) Still... I managed to get a part-time
job at the Museum. That's why I've got this mop and bucket. (*She displays
them*) Have you been there? The Museum. (*Impressed*) Oooh, it's ever so
interesting. Full of old pottery and statues of folks with no clothes on.
Here... (*confidentially*) and you should see some of those *foreign* ones.
They brought a new one in this morning. "David" by Michaelangelo.
Ooooooh. It made my mou... (*hastily correcting herself*) eyes water, just
looking at it. Talk about *filthy*. They must have pigeons the size of
elephants in Italy. Anyway... The Head cleaner took one look at it and told
me I'd have to help her give it a good scrubbing to clean it up again. "You
take the back", she said, "and I'll do the front". "Well", I said, "I don't think
that's fair. You're getting the best job". "No, I'm not", she said, "There's
a lot more marble at the front, so there's more for me to clean". "I know",
I said, "but at least you've got somewhere to hang your bucket".

*There is the sound of merriment off UL, and Princess Rosamund dances
happily on to the stage in the company of several laughing friends. She is
a very attractive girl of twenty, and wears a costume similar in fashion to
those of her companions. Catching sight of Dame Lovelorn, she stops dead
in her tracks, looking dismayed*

(*Recognizing her and dropping her mop and bucket in shock*) Rosamund.
Princess (*nervously*) Dame Lovelorn. What are *you* doing here?

Her companions fall silent and look puzzled

Dame (*gaping*) Never mind *me*. What about *you*? (*She looks at the others*)
And who are this lot? Riverdance [or famous pop group]? (*To them*) Go
away. Get out of it. Shoo. Shoo.

*They look baffled, shrug, then exit as Rosamund hurries down to her,
contritely*

Princess Oh, please don't be angry with me. I know you said I was never to
leave the forest but King Pat-a-cake's going to make a Royal Announcement
and all three of the Princes will be here for it. I only wanted to see what they
looked like.

Dame (*concernedly*) Yes. And now everybody'll know what *you* look like, as well. (*Anguished*) Oh, whatever are we going to do? As soon as Queen Venoma finds out *this* is where we've been hiding, she'll have *you* married to that ugly son of hers and *I'll* be chained up in her dungeons till the *next* millennium. (*Horrified*) Ohhhhh. I'll be almost thirty before I'm out again. (*She looks stricken*)

Princess (*comforting her*) Don't worry, Dame Lovelorn. No-one knows who I *really* am, and even if they *did*, I'm sure they'd never tell her.

Dame (*scornfully*) Wouldn't they? And what about him down there, then? (*She indicates into the audience*) The Mayor of [local town]. He'd tell folks *anything*, he would. (*She glares into the audience*)

Princess (*looking*) Really?

Dame I wouldn't trust him as far as I could throw him. Five hundred pounds he offered me last Christmas. Just to let him kiss me under the mistletoe. I couldn't believe my ears. *Five hundred pounds* for a kiss. (*She looks indignant*)

Princess (*wide-eyed*) And what did you do?

Dame Well… (*She glances around to ensure no-one can overhear*) There was nobody else around … and with it being Christmas I *had* had a drin… (*Hastily correcting herself*) I mean… I was feeling a bit *charitable* … so I told him to go ahead. Oh, Rosamund. *It was the biggest mistake of my life.* The minute he came up for air, I asked him for the five hundred and do you know what he said to me? (*Firmly*) "Go jump in the lake for it".

Princess (*shocked*) But that's *terrible*.

Dame I know. And by the time I got back again he'd gone. (*She remembers*) Anyway … never mind about that. We can't stay here any longer. (*She picks up her mop and bucket*) Just wait till I take these back, then it's straight home for us so we can start packing.

Princess (*sadly*) Do we *really* have to leave, Dame Lovelorn? I've hardly met another person since the day I was born. And as for *boys*…

Dame (*startled*) Boys? At your age you shouldn't even know what a boy is.

Princess (*protesting*) But I've got to meet one *some* day. How else will I be able to marry?

Dame (*relenting*) Oh, don't worry, Rosamund. As soon as Prince Ghastly's found somebody else to marry, you'll be able to meet anyone you like. Now just wait here till I get back and don't let anyone see you.

Dame Lovelorn exits L

Princess (*dejectedly*) Don't let anyone see you. How many times has she told me that? I must be the only girl in the world who's never had the chance to fall in love. (*She sighs deeply*) Oh, if only life were like the stories in the books I've read. I'm sure *some* handsome young man would arrive to sweep me off my feet.

No. 2 Song (Princess Rosamund)

At the end of the song Rosamund exits DR, *sadly*

There is a commotion off L *and Peter Piper's voice is heard calling anxiously*

Peter (*off*) Woa ... woa. Come back. Somebody stop him. Woaaaaa.

To a few bars of jolly music, Peglegasus the horse comes gambolling on to the stage UL *and executes an anti-clockwise circuit using the whole area and thoroughly enjoying himself*

A harrassed looking Peter enters UL, *and runs* UC, *looking off* R. *He is the Royal Groom, but looks more like a jockey in his short-legged breeches, oversized boots, striped stockings and garish shirt. He carries a length of stout rope and is totally unaware that Peglegasus is now behind him*

(*Calling off* R) Come back you rotten old gee-gee. Where do you think you're going?

Peglegasus completes his circuit by crashing into Peter's back and sending him sprawling. Peter drops the rope

Owwwwwww.

Peglegasus faces the audience and shakes with laughter as Peter scrambles to his feet

(*Annoyed*) I suppose you think that's *funny*?

Peglegasus nods happily

Yes. Well, it *isn't*. You're a naught naughty, naughty old horse.

Peglegasus shakes his head in denial

(*Firmly*) Oh, yes, you are.

Peglegasus shakes his head again

(*Wagging his finger sternly*) Oh, yes, you are.

Peglegasus tosses his head to the audience, inviting them to join in and shakes his head again. When the audience responds, Peter notices them for the first time

Ohhh. Hallo. (*He gives an embarrassed laugh*) I didn't notice you lot out there. (*He moves* DC *to speak to them*) I was talking to the horse. (*He indicates the horse, awkwardly*) Peglegasus.

Peglegasus nudges him and whispers

(*To the horse*) Eh? (*He listens again*) Oh, all right. (*To the audience*) He says I've to tell you he was named after the famous flying horse in Ancient Greece.

Peglegasus nods proudly and bows for applause

But he's so old, I bet it wasn't *long* after. (*He chortles with delight and turns his back to Peglegasus as he doubles up with laughter, clutching his stomach*)

Peglegasus quivers with annoyance, then turns his back and kicks him on the bottom

(*Pained*) Owwwww. (*He spins round*) Ooooooh, you naughty, naughty, naughty, naughty horse.

Peglegasus swaggers away L

(*Peeved*) That's the last time I'm going for a walk with *you*. (*To the audience as he rubs his aching bottom*) It's bad enough having to carry a poop scoop when I take the *corgies* out. I need a dumper truck for *him*. Talk about *embarrassing*. He does it *anywhere*. They won't let us through the *door* at [local supermarket] these days. Mind you ... it's all organic, isn't it? And that's the thing today. We've had enough of these Geriatric'lly Mollified foods, haven't we? Yes. It's all natural, chemical-free, *healthy* stuff we want now. There's a feller down our street won't eat anything *but* organic food. A vegetarian, he is. Runner beans for breakfast ... lettuce and cucumber for lunch ... peas, carrots and broccoli for dinner ... and brussel sprouts for supper. He went into hospital last week with a bad attack of white-fly. (*He chortles*) Mind you ... there's still *some* folks who know nothing about organics, isn't there? I was passing 10 Downing Street this morning when the door opened and out came [Prime Minister's wife]. "What on earth do you do with all that horse manure you keep collecting," she said. "Well", I told her "King Pat-a-cake likes me to put it on his rhubarb". "Good Heavens", she said. "[Prime Minister's forename] always has custard on *his*." (*He grins*) Anyway ... I'd better introduce meself, hadn't I? My name's Peter Piper, and I look after all the horses in the Royal Stables. (*He throws a glance at Peglegasus*) Including that one over there. The only trouble is, I've got so much work to do, I never get time to make any friends, so I'm always *lonely*.

He looks dejected until the audience responds

Oh, I'm lonelier than *that*.

The audience responds louder

Blimey. I'm not *that* lonely. No. No. I just need somebody to *talk* to now and then. Somebody to have a *laugh* with. (*He has an idea*) Here ... just a minute. There's lots of boys and girls out there, so *you* can be my friends, can't you?

Audience response

Yes. Of course you can. So I'll tell you what we'll do. Every time I come on, I'll shout "Hiya, kids" and you can shout back "Hiya, Peter" at the top of your voices. Will you do that for me? Will you?

Audience response

You don't sound too sure about it. But never mind. We'll have a little practice first ... just to see you get it right. I'll go off and come back on again, and when I shout "Hiya, kids", you shout back "Hiya, Peter" as loud as you can. OK? I'm going then.

Peter hurries off R ... *then returns*

Hiya, Kids.

Audience response

Ooooooh—is that the best you can do? My *tummy* can rumble louder than *that*. No, no, no. I want you to *scream* the place down. Let 'em hear you in [next town or village]. Let's try it again.

He "rehearses" with the audience until satisfied

Right. Well, now we're all friends, I'd better get back to the castle with

Peglegasus, before they realize we're missing. But I'll see you later. (*He glances round*) Now where's me rope gone? (*He locates it and picks it up*) Come on, Peglegasus. Home we go. (*He puts the rope round Peglegasus's neck*) You're going to have a nice clean stable waiting for you, aren't you?

Peglegasus nods

And a big bunch of juicy fresh carrots.

Peglegasus nods again

Some lovely, sweet, rosy-red apples.

Peglegasus nods faster

And after you've eaten all *those*, we can trot you all the way down to the vet's for your yearly injection.

Peglegasus nods again, then realizing, quickly changes it to a vigorous shake of his head

As Peter looks surprised, Peglegasus pulls the rope out of his hand and dashes off R

(*Startled*) Here. Come back.

Peter races off in pursuit, shouting, then almost at once backs on to the stage again, pulling on the end of the rope

(*Struggling with it*) Woa. Woa.

A tug of war commences with the absent horse

A Citizen enters UL to see the battle

(*Anxiously*) He's getting away again. Help me. Help me.

Hurrying to Peter, the Citizen takes hold of the rope in front of Peter and pulls

As they drag more rope on to the stage, other Citizens enter and also grab hold, all shouting encouragement

Peter remains at the rear. Still pulling, Peter backs offstage L and into the

*wings, gradually followed by the crowd still attempting to haul Peglegasus
back on to the stage. The struggle continues until all have exited, still
calling and panting. As the last one vanishes from view, Peter enters R at
the other end of the rope, and is pulled L*

(*Cheerily*) Hiya, kids.

Peter exits L on the end of the rope, waving

*A loud fanfare is heard and Ambrose enters DR, followed by excited
Citizens from L and R*

Ambrose (*moving C and announcing*) His Royal Majesty, King Pat-a-cake
the Prodigious.

*As the crowd cheer loudly, King Pat-a-cake enters DR and moves DC,
beaming happily and giving royal waves to them*

Ambrose follows him DL

King (*happily*) Right, Lord Chamberlain. Have the Princes been summoned?
Ambrose Indeed they have, Sire. And here they come now.

*The King and Ambrose move slightly L as another fanfare signals the
entrance of Prince Fyne and Prince Dandi, UR. They are an odd matched
pair, and although richly dressed and wearing small crowns, are not
exactly over-endowed with intelligence. They move DC as the crowd
pointedly ignore them*

King (*beaming*) Ah, my two favourite children. Prince Fyne and Prince
Dandi. (*Puzzled*) But where's Prince Peerless?
Fyne (*disgustedly*) Don't ask *us*. We've been sitting in [local hospital] all
morning.
King (*alarmed*) Good Heavens. Whatever for?
Dandi (*miserably*) I'd just finished putting my shirt on when I got this terrible
pain in my neck and couldn't breathe properly. I thought I was going to die.
King (*anxiously*) And what did the doctor say?
Fyne He'd put his head through one of the buttonholes. (*He chortles*)

The Citizens look amused

Dandi (*peeved*) Yes. Well, *you've* some need to poke fun. Look at the time
you had the royal chihuahua trained to come for his food whenever you
rang a bell.

Fyne And what was wrong with that?
Dandi The first time it heard one, it ate two boxes of biscuits, ten pounds of
steak and a door-to-door salesman.

The Citizens react again

King (*hastily*) Boys. Boys. Boys. This is no time for arguing. I'm about to
make a very important announcement.
Fyne Well, I hope it's a quick one. They're coming to empty the swimming
pool again this afternoon.
King What? (*He protests*) But we've only just had it installed.
Fyne I know. But somebody filled it with fizzy lemonade instead of water
and every time I swallow some, it tires me out. I can't even manage a
length.
King (*puzzled*) Why ever not?
Fyne I swim two strokes forward, burp, and shoot back *five*.

The Citizens are amused

Dandi And *I'm* in a hurry as well 'cos I'm going round to my girlfriend's in
a few minutes' time. (*Coyly*) I bought a present for her yesterday.
Ambrose (*beaming*) Oh, how romantic. And, er ... what exactly *is* it, Your
Highness?
Dandi (*smugly*) A bottle of Elizabeth Taylor's world famous toilet water.
One hundred pounds it cost me. (*He glances around for approval*)
Fyne (*amazed*) One hundred pounds? (*To the others*) I always knew he was
crackers. He could have got it for *nothing* out of ours.

The princes glower at each other

King (*hastily*) Boys. Boys. (*He looks around in annoyance*) Where *is* Prince
Peerless? We can't wait about all *day* for him.
Ambrose (*glancing off* UR) Here he comes now, Your Majesty.

*There is a fanfare and Prince Peerless enters UR. He is the youngest and
most handsome of the princes. Intelligent and kind, he wears a plain,
belted, brown tunic over an orange ballet-sleeved shirt, dark tights, and a
money pouch is tucked into his belt. There is no crown on his head*

As the crowd greet him, he moves DC. The two other princes move R in disgust

King (*slightly peeved*) At last.
Peerless (*apologetically*) Sorry, I'm late, Father. I didn't mean to keep you
waiting.

King (*sternly*) I should hope not indeed. (*He looks him up and down in surprise*) But why are you dressed like *that*? And where's your Royal Crown?

Peerless I didn't see the point in wearing it, Father. I've been helping the animals all morning. Down on the Royal Farm.

King (*taken aback*) Helping the animals?

Peerless One of the sheepdogs hurt its leg, so I rounded up the sheep for it. Then the cows needed milking, so I did *that* for them ... the pigs wanted their sty cleaning and I did *that* for them ... and some of the hens weren't feeling too well, so——

Fyne (*interupting*) Don't tell us. You laid the *eggs* for them.

Fyne and Dandi laugh mockingly

King (*ignoring them*) Oh, well. Now we're all here, we can make a start. (*To Ambrose*) Off you go, Lord Chamberlain.

Ambrose looks confused then turns to exit

(*Hastily*) No, no. I mean read them the *announcement*.

Ambrose (*realizing*) Oh, yes, Sire. Of course. (*He produces a large scroll from the inside of his gown and after unrolling it, reads out the announcement*)

Everyone reacts as the announcement is made

By order of His Royal Majesty, King Pat-a-cake the Prodigious, let it hereby be known that in order to name his successor as Ruler of Euphoria, it is decreed that whichever prince can discover the hiding place of a certain wonderful treasure, namely the Golden Net, then that prince will inherit the throne on day of his return. (*He re-rolls the scroll*)

Dandi (*baffled*) Golden Net? And what's *that* when it's at home?

Fyne (*blankly*) Never heard of it

Peerless (*puzzled*) Neither have I.

King (*gleefully*) No, but *I* have. (*In awed tones*) It's a net so large it can hold the entire world in its meshes, yet so fine it can be drawn through the tiniest wedding ring ever made.

Fyne (*amazed*) What'cha wanna thing like that for? That lot in Brussels'll never let you go fishing with it. Stick to your quota, they'll tell you.

Dandi And how do we carry it if we *do* find it?

King (*firmly*) That's *your* problem. All *I* know is I want that Golden Net, and the first one to bring it to me will be the next King. (*To the crowd*) Right. That's it. The Royal Announcement's over. You can all go home now. (*To*

Ambrose, happily) Come along, Ambrose. It's nearly time for [children's TV programme] and I mustn't miss *that*, must I?

The King and Ambrose exit L, discussing the programme

Peerless (*dreamily*) The Golden Net. So large it can contain the earth, yet so fine it can be drawn through a wedding ring. (*He snaps out of it*) But where do we start to look for it? Perhaps someone here can help us? I can't *wait* to set eyes on it. (*He eagerly moves to the Citizens and chats silently*)

Fyne (*aside to Dandi*) No. And neither can we. We're not letting *him* get his hands on this Golden Net. If anyone's having that crown, it's going to be one of *us*.

Dandi You're right. Quick. Back to the castle. If we get there first, we can grab the best horses and be off before he knows we've gone.

Fyne (*sniggering*) And by that time he won't stand a *chance* of catching up with us. (*Smugly*) Look out, Golden Net. Here we come.

Furtively, Fyne and Dandi hurry off L

Peerless (*turning to speak to his brothers*) Well, no-one *here* seems to have heard of it, but… (*Surprised*) Oh. (*He glances around*) They've gone.

Citizen 1 Yes. And if *we* know them as well as we *think* we know them, they'll be hoping to get a head start on you.

Citizen 2 But don't worry, Peerless. When brains were given out, those two were *definitely* last in the line. If anyone finds the Golden Net, it won't be them.

Citizen 3 And as far as *we're* concerned, the next King of Euphoria is going to be you.

All agree

Peerless (*unhappily*) That's all very well, but I haven't a *clue* where this wonderful Net could be hidden. Looks like I'll just have to search the world for it and hope for the best. (*He brightens up*) But with all my friends to cheer me on my way, whatever the future has in store for me, I'll face it with a smile and a song.

No. 3 Song (Peerless and Chorus)

At the end of the song, Peerless exits UL with Citizens forming a tableau to wave him goodbye

The Lights fade to Black-out

SCENE 2

A Forest Path

A lane scene. The backdrop depicts the depths of an ancient forest

Dappled lighting

Mother Goose enters R, *followed by her goose, Ghiselle*

Mother Goose (*beaming*) Well, my dears, how's that
    For something off the beaten track?
    But what occurs, I hear you think,
    Before those Princes three get back?
    Well, sure as eggs, it's safe to say that even as I'm speaking,
    Queen Venoma is casting spells to find the fair Princess she's
    seeking.
    As for the rest, I recommend you simply to "sit tight";
    And everything will be revealed before I bid you all "Good-
    night".

*Giving a broad wink to the audience, Mother Goose crosses Ghiselle and
exits* R, *with Ghiselle following her*

The Lights brighten slightly and Dame Lovelorn hurries on L *in another
colourful costume*

Dame (*clutching at her heart*) Oh, boys and girls. I've nearly had a
conniption. There's been a fellow following me ... all the way through the
forest. I walked ever so slow, but he wouldn't catch up. In the end I had to
go back and speak to him and you'll never guess what he wanted.
(*Indignantly*) To sell me a ticket for a [famous pop star] concert. "On your
way, chum", I said. "I'm not paying good money to listen to rubbish like
him". "Rubbish?" he said. "*Rubbish*? He's one of the world's biggest stars.
Have you never heard him sing?" "No", I said, "but I heard a feller in [local
pub or club] last night *imitating* him, and *he* sounded *terrible*." Anyway
... I'm not into live theatre any more. Not since I went to see a play at [local
theatre]. Fifteen pounds it cost me for a seat and I only saw the first act
before I walked out. Well ... the programme said "Act Two: Five years
later" ... and I wasn't going to wait *that* long.

Peter Piper enters L

Peter (*to the audience*) Hiya, kids.

Audience response

Here, you'll never guess what's happened. Old King Pat-a-cake's... (*He notices the Dame*) Oh. Hallo. I didn't know there was anybody else here.

Dame (*frostily*) Well, I noticed that much. Who are *you*?

Peter Peter Piper. The Royal Groom.

Dame (*impressed and softening*) Oh, I say. (*Curious*) And what are you doing out here, then? In the middle of the forest?

Peter Trying to catch up with Prince Peerless. Him and his two brothers are trying to find the Golden Net, but *they* took all the horses and left *him* to walk. He must be worn out by now. It's over twenty miles from the castle, and it's taken *me* five minutes to get here.

Dame Hang on a bit. You can't walk twenty miles in five minutes.

Peter Not usually, but I know a short cut.

Dame (*after a reaction*) And what are you going to do when you find him?

Peter Keep him company, of course. He can't walk about on his own. Not a *prince*. If he wants to be on his own, he has to have somebody with him.

Dame Not if he lived in Scotland, he wouldn't. Bonny Prince Charlie once walked into an hotel in Glasgow all on his own, had a drink at the bar, a four course dinner in the restaurant and then asked the manager for a tartan room.

Peter And did he get one?

Dame He got 'em *both*. Anyway ... never mind all that. I, er ... I'm glad I met *you*, because you *might* be able to do me a *favour*. (*She simpers at him*)

Peter (*warily*) Favour?

Dame Yes. I'm a bit short of money, so I was wondering if you could lend me thirty pounds till I get my Winter Fuel Allowance?

Peter (*taken aback*) Thirty pounds? But we've only just met. (*Uncomfortable*) Oh, all right. (*He gets his pouch purse out and extracts three ten pound notes*) Here you are. But I want it back, you know. (*He gives her the money*)

Dame Well, of course you do. I won't *forget*. (*Patiently*) *I* owe *you* thirty pounds. Bye bye. (*She turns to exit*)

Peter (*looking into his empty purse*) Here ... wait a minute. I've given you *all* my money, now. I've got nothing left.

Dame (*turning back*) Oh, I say... You can't be left with *nothing*. (*She thinks quickly*) I'll tell you what I'll do. I'll *lend* you ten pounds. All right? (*She gives him ten pounds*) There. Now *you* owe me ten pounds and *I* owe you twenty.

Peter (*relieved*) Right.

Dame (*thinking again*) But if I give you the twenty pounds *I* owe *you*... (*she gives him the notes*) and *you* give me the ten you owe *me*... (*she takes it out of his hand*) we'll both be even, won't we? Lovely. (*She beams and turns away again*)

Peter (*quickly*) Er ... just a minute. Just a minute. I think we've got this wrong.

Dame (*turning back*) Wrong? What do you mean, wrong? (*She takes the twenty pounds off him*) Look. You stand over here and pretend to be *me*, and I'll stand over there and pretend to be *you*.

They change sides

Now then. *You* ask *me* to lend you thirty pounds. (*She nods for him to proceed*)

Peter (*after some preparation*) Excuse me. Will you lend me thirty pounds?

Dame (*sweetly*) Of course I will, young man. Here you are. (*She hands over the money*) Ten ... twenty ... thirty pounds. Right? (*She beams at him*)

Peter Right. Now *I* owe *you*, thirty pounds?

Dame That's right. Now if you lend me *ten*.

Peter (*handing it over*) Ten pounds.

Dame (*taking it*) Then *I* owe *you* ten pounds, and *you* owe *me* twenty. See?

Peter (*slowly*) Yes.

Dame (*patiently*) Now then ... if I give you the ten I owe you (*she does so*) and you give me the twenty you owe me (*she takes it*) that means we don't owe each other anything, doesn't it? Dead simple. (*She turns to go*)

Peter (*to himself*) I think I must be. (*Annoyed*) Wait a minute. Wait. It doesn't make *sense*. It's all *wrong*.

Dame (*turning back, exasperated*) It's not all wrong. How can it be? Ooooh, I'm beginning to wish we'd never started this. (*Very patiently*) Look. The only reason it doesn't make sense, is because *you're* on the wrong side. Change places again.

They do so and she takes the ten pound note from him

Now then. (*She waves the thirty pounds*) I've got the money, haven't I? All thirty pounds of it.

Peter Yes.

Dame Now *you* ask *me* if you can borrow it. (*She indicates for him to go ahead*)

Peter (*through gritted teeth*) Will you lend me thirty pounds?

Dame (*she counts as she hands over the money*) Ten ... twenty ... thirty pounds. Right?

Peter Right.

Dame So how much do you owe me?

Peter Thirty pounds.

Dame And you're quite *sure* about that?

Peter Of course I am. I've got it right here. (*He waves the money*)

Dame (*tartly*) Good. Well, in that case, I'd better have it back before you spend it all. (*She takes the money out of his hand*) And don't come borrowing money again. It's a very nasty habit.

Dame Lovelorn exits rapidly R

Peter (*to the audience; ruefully*) She's right, kids, you should never borr... (*He suddenly realizes*) Here... (*He calls after her*) Come back. Wait.

Peter hurriedly exits R, *still shouting*

The Lights dim and Venoma appears L *in a green follow spot, and holding a crystal ball*

Venoma   (*glaring into the ball*) Within thy depths, all secrets lie,
And what is hidden, is revealed.
So show me *now*, dear crystal globe,
Where Nurse and Princess are concealed.

She stares fixedly into the globe for a few seconds, then her face contorts in anger

Nothing. Still nothing. Yet I *know* this cursed country hides them both. (*Hissing*) What power protects them? Who dares to defy the will of Queen Venoma? By the crooked toes of the Great Green Goblin, I shall seek them out and... (*She stops suddenly*) Wait. Wait. Only one Immortal being has the skill to cloud my crystal. That interferring old hag, *Mother Goose*. (*In a fury*) Confound her. Is my quest, then, to end in failure? (*Recovering herself*) No. *No*. In spite of *all* her magic spells, Queen Venoma shall win the game. (*Clutching the crystal ball tightly, she casts a spell*)
Creatures of the forest, small. Night owls, in the treetops tall.
Things that spin, or flap or crawl, upon your help I now do call.
Where'er the missing princess be, her whereabouts report to *me*,
And come the dawn or eventide, my darling son shall claim his bride.

With a cackling shriek of laughter, Venoma exits L, *as the scene ends in a rapid fade*

SCENE 3

Dame Lovelorn's Cottage Garden

A full set. A cheerful garden backdrop, crowded with hollyhocks, lupins, roses, etc. Part of the cottage itself can be seen R, and is thatched, half-timbered, brightly coloured, and smothered with window boxes, climbing roses and ivys, etc. It has a practical door. Blossoming trees hide entrances and exits, and a small rustic bench is DL. The whole effect should be charming

When the scene begins, dancers dressed as colourful butterflies and/or other insects, perform a graceful dance

No. 4 Dance (Butterflies and Other Insects)

At the end of the dance, all exit L and R

A bedraggled Prince Dandi totters on UL, followed by an equally dishevelled Prince Fyne

Dandi (*delightedly*) Look. A cottage. We're saved. We're saved. (*He begins to move towards the cottage*)

Fyne (*grabbing him*) Just a minute. Just a minute. What are you *doing*?

Dandi (*surprised*) I'm going to knock on the door and find out where we are.

Fyne Are you crackers? We don't want folks to see us like *this*. We look like a couple of tramps.

Dandi Well, what do you expect? We've been lost in that forest for hours.

Fyne Yes. And whose fault was *that*, eh? If you'd tied the horses up properly, none of this would have happened and we wouldn't have to pay for them when we get home again.

Dandi (*blankly*) Why should we have to pay for 'em?

Fyne Because they're Government property, of course, and all Government property has to be paid for when it gets lost.

Dandi (*scornfully*) Give over.

Fyne I'm telling you. If you were in the army and lost your rifle, they'd take *five hundred pounds* out of your wages to pay for it. And if you were in the Air Force and lost your parachute, they'd take a *thousand* pounds.

Dandi What about the Navy?

Fyne Same thing. If you lose something, they stop it out of your wages.

Dandi Blimey. No wonder the captain goes down with his ship.

Fyne (*pushing him*) Ooooh. You know what *your* trouble is, don't you?

Dandi What? What?

Fyne You're *stupid*.

Dandi (*indignantly*) No, I'm not. I have dreams every night, I do.

Fyne (*baffled*) What are you talking about? Dreams every night. What have dreams got to do with not being stupid?

Dandi It was in the *Sunday Sport* last month. Only *intelligent* people dream, it said. (*Cockily*) So ... if I have a dream every night I can't be stupid, can I?

Fyne Well, what do you dream about?

Dandi (*excitedly*) Cricket matches, of course. I just *love* cricket matches. Every night I'm there at Lords with all the world's best players, batting and bowling, running and catching. Night after night after night. (*Dreamily*) Just one long match after another.

Fyne (*in disbelief*) And that's all you dream about? Cricket?

Dandi (*happily*) Yes.

Fyne Don't you ever dream about horse-racing ... or water-skiing ... or girls?

Dandi What ... and miss my innings? Anyway ... what about *you*, Mr Perfect? I bet *you* don't dream, do you?

Fyne (*defensively*) Course I do. I was dreaming last night. Mind you ... if I carry on having dreams like the one I had last night, I shall have to go see the doctor.

Dandi (*wide eyed*) Why? What did you dream about?

Fyne I dreamed I was James Bond ... and I was trapped on a desert island with hundreds and hundreds of beautiful girls ... every one of them wanting to make passionate love to me. I was pushing them away and pushing them away but they still kept coming at me. (*Almost tearfully*) And I pushed and I pushed and I pushed...

Dandi And what do you want the doctor to do? Stop you dreaming?

Fyne No, you fathead—I want him to break my arms. (*He chortles*)

Dandi (*peeved*) Oh, go on. Go on. Make fun of me. But just you wait till I find this Golden Net thing, and they make me King of Euphoria. You'll be laughing on the other side of your face.

Fyne (*amused*) King of Euphoria? You? Don't be daft. There's only one feller they'll be giving the crown to, and that's me. (*He puts his arm around Dandi's shoulders*) But never mind. We'll still be best mates, and from then on there'll only be good times for both of us.

No. 5 Song (Fyne and Dandi)

As the song ends, Fyne and Dandi exit into the cottage

Dame Lovelorn enters L *... wearing another outrageous outfit, and moves* DC

Dame Do you like the outfit, girls? (*She parades it*) I bought it in [local dress shop]. They were having a sale, and everybody who bought something got a free gift. Yes. Mine was a new kind of bra. I'm wearing it now. It's called "The Sheepdog Bra". It sort of rounds 'em up and points 'em in the right direction. (*She adjusts her bust*) Mind you... I shouldn't have been buying new clothes at all. Not with having to pack everything and move house again. Trouble was, I needed it for the funeral I've just been to. Well... I don't usually go to funerals, but I'd known this feller for years. He was the chap who invented the Hokey Cokey. Ooooh, and what a carry on. They hadn't made the grave big enough and they couldn't get the coffin to fit. It was in, out, in, out, shake it all about... And the poor feller's *brother*. All the way from Scotland, *he'd* come, and they kicked him out of the cemetery for crying. Well ... not *exactly* for crying... He kept wiping his eyes with the hem of his kilt.

The Princess enters from the cottage

Princess Dame Lovelorn. (*She hurries down to her*) Thank goodness you're home again. Two strange men are inside the cottage.
Dame (*startled*) Eh?
Princess I heard them arrive a few minutes ago, so I hid in the wardrobe.
Dame Ooo-er. (*Concerned*) They've not come about the Census, have they?
Princess (*puzzled*) Census?
Dame (*nodding*) Yes. They come about it every few years. You have to fill in a form to tell 'em how many of you are living in the house and other daft questions. I remember the *last* one I got. "State the length of your residence in this country", it said.
Princess And what did you write?
Dame Thirty-six feet, nine inches ... with a garage at the side.
Princess (*glancing anxiously at the cottage*) What are we going to do?
Dame Don't worry about it. You hide in the garden, and I'll get rid of 'em. As soon as they're gone, we'll catch the next coach out of here. (*She chortles*) By this time tomorrow, we'll be miles away and Venoma will never find us.
Princess But where will we go?
Dame Well ... if the [political party] are still in charge, we can go to Great Britain, then the *next* time we have to move, we'll be worth a small fortune.
Princess Why's that?
Dame We'll be going there with a *big* fortune. Now stop asking questions and hide.

Rosamund hurries off DL *and the Dame exits into the cottage*

Prince Peerless enters UL, *carrying a horseshoe*

Peerless (*looking round in surprise*) A garden. In the middle of the forest.

And a cottage, too. (*Relieved*) Thank goodness for that. Now at least I can find out where I am and if anyone's seen my brothers. But I wonder who lives there? So far away from the city. (*Brightly*) Well, there's only one way to find out. (*He moves towards the cottage door*)

Peter enters L

Peter Hiya, kids.

Audience response

Peerless (*turning in surprise*) Peter. What are *you* doing here?

Peter I thought you might be needing a bit of help. But cor, you don't half move fast for a feller in high heels.

Peerless (*ruefully*) I suppose I *have* been hurrying, but I was trying to catch up with Fyne and Dandi. (*Dejectedly*) It's no use, though. I've not seen a sign of them for hours. (*Brightening*) However... I *did* find this *horseshoe*, (*he shows the horseshoe*) and you know what *that* means, don't you?

Peter Course I do. There's a horse running round in its socks.

Peerless (*amused*) No, no, no. It means that they can't be too far ahead. You can't ride a horse with a missing shoe, so before they can go any further they'll need to have a new one fitted. Whoever lives in this cottage may be able to tell us how far it is to the nearest blacksmith's.

Peter (*excitedly*) Hey. You're right. (*He grimaces*) Pity it isn't my Uncle Fred's cottage, 'cos he knew where everything was. Mind you ... he wasn't very nice and he was always in trouble.

Peerless (*surprised*) Really?

Peter Yes. He fell out with everybody. Two minutes after you'd met him, you'd be fighting hammer and tongs. He once bit a chunk out of another feller's *ear*.

Peerless (*shocked*) What?

Peter Yes. And when the Magistrates ordered him to keep the peace, he said it was too late. He'd already swallowed it.

Peerless Well ... perhaps we're better off *not* meeting your uncle. (*Briskly*) But there's no time to lose if we're to pass those sneaky brothers of mine and find this mysterious Golden Net. Without it, I don't stand a chance of becoming King of Euphoria.

Peter Right. Well, you have a sit down and rest your feet while I find out if anybody's passed here lately. (*He moves to the cottage door and knocks*)

Peerless sits on the rustic bench and puts the horseshoe down on it

(*Calling*) Come out. Come out, whoever you are.

There is no answer, and he knocks again

(*Calling*) Coo-ee? Is anybody there?

As there is still no answer, he peers through the window, but seeing nothing, exits behind the cottage as though looking for signs of life

Peerless gently rubs his foot

Rosamund cautiously appears LC *behind the bench, and without noticing Peerless, moves towards the cottage*

As Peerless straightens, he catches sight of her and rises

Peerless Hallo.
Princess (*startled*) Oh. (*She spins to face him, then backs away*)
Peerless (*hastily*) Wait. There's nothing to be afraid of.

Rosamund pauses

(*Bowing deeply*) Prince Peerless of Euphoria, at your service.
Princess (*surprised*) Prince Peerless? But ... what are you doing *here*? In the middle of the forest.
Peerless Searching for a hidden treasure. Though to tell the truth, I believe that I've already found it.
Princess (*puzzled*) I don't understand.
Peerless (*gallantly*) You're the most beautiful girl I've ever seen ... and I don't even know who you are.
Princess (*thinking quickly*) No-one at all. I'm just a peasant girl. Now please ... leave here at once and forget that you ever saw me.
Peerless (*puzzled*) But why?
Princess Because no-one must know that I'm here. It's a closely guarded secret.
Peerless Now *I* don't understand.
Princess Oh, please don't ask me to explain. It's much too complicated. (*She hesitates*) But ... you can tell me about the *treasure* you're seeking. What *is* it?
Peerless (*grimacing*) A Golden Net. So large it can encompass the world, yet so fine it could be drawn through the smallest wedding ring. (*Wryly*) Though where to start looking for it, I haven't a clue.

Rosamund laughs merrily

Don't you believe me?

Princess Of course. But isn't the treasure you're seeking, the same one we *all* want?

Peerless (*puzzled*) I'm sorry.

Princess One doesn't have to *search* for it. When the time is right, the Golden Net comes to you. (*Patiently*) It's just another name for "love".

Peerless (*doubtfully*) Are you sure?

Princess (*laughing*) Well, of course I am. My nursemaid told me *that* when I was only a child.

Peerless (*dazedly to himself*) Then... I've already *found* it And the Crown of Euphoria's mine. (*To Rosamund, happily*) I don't know your name, or even why you're hiding, but once I've told my father the good news, I'll be returning to ask for your hand in marriage. If *I'm* to be King of Euphoria, then no-one but *you* shall be my Queen.

Princess (*startled*) But I *can't*. It's impossible. And even if it weren't, we've only just met. You can't possibly be in love with me.

Peerless That's just where you're wrong. And if you'll give me a little time I'll prove it to you.

No. 6 Song (Peerless and Rosamund)

At the end of the song, Peter hurries on UR *and dashes past Rosamund without noticing her*

Peter (*to the audience*) Hiya, kids.

Audience response as he grabs hold of Prince Peerless's sleeve

Quick. Quick. We've got to get back to Euphoria.

Peerless (*startled*) What's the hurry?

Peter (*frantically*) I know what the Golden Net is.

Peerless (*happily*) So do I. This beautiful lady's (*he indicates the Princess*) just told me.

Peter turns and sees her, smiles and nods, then turns back to Peerless

Peter Yes. And the ugly old one in *there* (*he indicates the cottage*) 's just told Fyne and Dandi. They're heading back to the castle as fast as their legs can carry 'em. If they get there first you'll have had it.

Peerless (*alarmed*) Oh, no. (*To Rosamund*) I'll have to go. But I *will* be back. I promise.

Peerless and Peter hurry off UL, *leaving Rosamund gazing after them*

As the previous song music softly reprises, Rosamund sings the final few lines, then turns to exit R

The Lights dim and Venoma enters DL *in a green follow spot*

Venoma *(in commanding tones)* One moment.

Rosamund turns quickly and sees her

(Malevolently) So, my dear ... *this* is where you've been hiding yourself? How very *pleasant*.
Princess *(afraid)* Who *are* you?
Venoma *(sweetly)* Why ... the mother of your future husband, Prince Ghastly of Despondia.
Princess *(aghast)* Queen Venoma.

The Princess turns to run, but Venoma quickly casts a spell and she is halted

Venoma   *(approaching her and purring)* How foolish your attempts to
                         flee
                    My darling son's strong arms.
                    How pitiful your schemes to hide
                    From all his myriad charms.
                    Your wedding day I'll now arrange;
                    The bridal feast prepare,
                    (Hissing) And by my troth, I promise you,
                    His life you'll ever share.
Princess *(protesting)* But how *can* I marry him? I've never even seen him.

Venoma produces a small framed photograph and hands it to her. The Princess gazes at it in horror, lets out a little scream, and drops it

I won't marry him. I won't. He's the ugliest person I've ever seen.
Venoma *(hissing)* Ugly or not. You'll be married at once. *(She seizes her arm)* Come. To the Castle of Despondia ... and the arms of your groom.

Venoma drags the protesting Rosamund off L

The green follow spot goes out

Dame Lovelorn hurries out of the cottage and DC

Dame *(anxiously looking round)* Rosamund? Where are you, dear? *(She*

sees the portrait on the ground) Oh ... somebody's dropped a picture graph.
(*She picks it up, looks at it and beams*) Oh, a little orangutan. Isn't that
sweet? I wonder where it got the crown from? (*She realizes*) Just a minute.
(*She peers at the picture again*) That's not an orangutan. It's Prince
Ghastly. (*Horrified*) Ohhhhhhh. They've got the Princess. Ohhhhh. Help.
Help.

Dame Lovelorn dashes off in a panic

Black-out

SCENE 4

A Corridor in Castle Splendid

A lane scene depicting the castle's interior

Mother Goose enters R *with Ghiselle*

Mother Goose (*shaking her head*) Oh, dear. Now *here's* a pretty mess:
            As clearly you've just seen.
            With things so black, it's time, I feel
            For *me* to intervene.
            (*Brightly*) With magic spoon and fairy charms
            Queen Venoma I'll thwart;
            And on the way, a lesson sharp
            I'll see she's quickly taught.
            So for awhile we've things to do
            My goose, Ghiselle and I,
            But never fear, we'll be back soon,
            Then watch the feathers fly.

Mother Goose chuckles and exits R, *followed by Ghiselle*

Ambrose enters L, *carrying a large blackboard*

Ambrose (*panting heavily*) Oh, dear, oh, dear, oh, dear. I shouldn't be
carrying things like this at my age. (*He deposits it* C, *and rests on it*) It's not
fair. I'm doing the work of three men, but I haven't been paid for ages.
(*Firmly*) The next time I see King Pat-a-cake, I'm going to ask him for
money.

The King enters L

King (*happily*) Ah, there you are, Ambrose. Good news. The three princes are on their way back and in a few more hours I can give up the throne and retire. (*He chuckles*) But I need a new hobby to keep me occupied. What do you suggest?

Ambrose Well... I suppose you could race pigeons, Your Majesty.

King Don't be silly, Ambrose. They'd fly much faster than *I* could run. (*He notices the blackboard*) Where are you going with that?

Ambrose Down to the kitchen, Sire. The chef wants to write tonight's menu on it.

King Oh. Well, tell him to make sure it's all *healthy* food. (*He crosses* R) Nothing too rich, you know. (*He heads for the exit*)

Ambrose Of course, Sire. But speaking of *rich*... I was wondering when I'd be getting my *wages*.

King (*startled*) Wages? (*He turns back*) What wages?

Ambrose For being the Lord Chamberlain. You promised me twenty pounds for every day worked and I haven't been paid for a year.

King Twenty pounds a day for a year? But that's, er ... er... (*He mentally adds up then gives a sigh of relief*) Oh, thank goodness for that. You had me worried for a moment. I don't owe you *anything*, do I? (*He smiles happily*)

Ambrose (*taken aback*) Don't you?

King Well, of course not. (*He chuckles*) And I'll prove it to you. (*He gets a stick of chalk from his pocket*) Now then... How many days are there in a year?

Ambrose Three hundred and sixty-five.

King And in a leap year?

Ambrose (*confused*) Oh, er ... er... (*He scratches his head*) I'll have to ask the audience.

Audience response

King Three hundred and sixty-six. So we'll write that down. (*He writes it on the blackboard*) Right. Now how many hours do you work in a day?

Ambrose Oh, eight hours, Your Majesty. Eight hours.

King Correct ... and as there's twenty-four hours in a day, you only *really* work a *third* of it, don't you?

Ambrose Er ... yes. I suppose so.

King Then if we divide three hundred and sixty-six by *three* (*he writes it on the board and turns to the audience*) that gives us?

Audience response

Exactly. One hundred and twenty-two. (*He writes it*)

Ambrose (*puzzled*) So I only work one hundred and twenty-two days a year?

King (*beaming*) No, no, no, no, no, Ambrose. Of course not. Nothing of the kind. You see ... you don't work Saturdays and Sundays, do you?

Ambrose (*indignantly*) Certainly *not*. No. No. I always have my Saturdays and Sundays off.

King And there are fifty-two Saturdays and fifty-two Sundays in a year, aren't there? And two fifty-twos are one hundred and four. So take one hundred and four away from one hundred and twenty-two. (*He does it on the board and turns to the audience again*) and we're left with?

Audience response

Perfectly right. Eighteen. (*He writes it on the board*)

Ambrose Oh, dear. (*He attempts to work it out in his head*)

King (*heartily*) Then of course ... you have *two weeks* holiday, don't you? Which is fourteen days. So if we take fourteen away from eighteen, (*he does it on the board*) there's only...

Audience response

...*four days left*. (*He writes it*)

Ambrose (*protesting*) But ... but...

King And we mustn't forget the four Bank Holidays, must we? So take four from four (*he does it on the board*) and we're left with *nothing*. (*He writes it on the board and beams triumphantly*)

Ambrose But that means I work all year and don't get a penny.

King That's true, I'm afraid. But luckily for me, I *do*. Because this isn't a leap year, is it? So *you* owe *me* one day's pay, which is twenty pounds exactly.

Ambrose But ... but ... I haven't got twenty pounds, Sire. I haven't got *anything*.

King (*kindly*) Well ... there's no need to worry. It isn't very much, so I'll take it out of your *next* year's wages. Bye bye.

King exits R, *followed by a protesting Ambrose, carrying the blackboard*

The Lights fade rapidly

SCENE 5

The Great Throne Room

A full set. A magnificent room in Castle Splendid, with a small dais UC, *on which the great throne is positioned. Lit by huge candelabra and chandeliers, the room is crowded with Guests, Courtiers, etc., all enjoying the hospitality of King Pat-a-cake*

No. 7 Song (Guests, Courtiers, etc.)

At the end of the song, Ambrose enters UR, *carrying his rod of office*

Ambrose (*announcing*) His Royal Majesty, King Pat-a-cake ... the Parsimonious.

As the King enters UR *in splendid new robes, and everyone gives deep bows and curtsies, the first few bars of "Colonel Bogey" are played*

The King reacts and glares at Ambrose, who looks innocent

King (*to the others*) Welcome to Castle Splendid and the magnificent party we're having to celebrate the return of the three princes with my beautiful Golden Net. (*He moves to sit on the throne*) Show them in at once, Lord Chamberlain.
Ambrose (*announcing*) Their Royal Highnesses, Prince Fyne, Prince Dandi and Prince Peerless.

A fanfare is sounded and all but the King bow and curtsy

Peter enters R

Peter Hiya, kids.

Audience response

King (*standing in surprise*) Who are *you*? You're not one of *my* sons.
Peter (*moving up to the throne*) That's right, Your Majesticals. I'm the Royal Groom, I am, and I've come to give you a message.
King (*put out*) Message? Who from? And why should *you* bring it? You're supposed to be looking after the horses, not delivering messages.
Peter (*indignantly*) Here... I've not always worked in the stables, you know. Before I came here I was a Government Artist.

King (*impressed*) Really? And what did you draw?

Peter Social Security. Sickness Benefit. Housing Benefit… (*He giggles*)

King (*irritated*) Ohhhhhh. What's the message?

Peter The message is … don't go giving the crown away till Prince Peerless gets back here.

King Prince Peerless? But where *is* he?

Peter Trying to help a feller who's dropped through an open trapdoor.

King (*startled*) Good Heavens. Was the poor man hurt?

Peter No. But he might have been if it hadn't been for the rope round his neck. (*He chortles*)

King (*fuming*) Ohhh. And what about my *other* sons, Fyne and Dandi?

Peter Don't worry about *them*, Your Hijesty. They'll be here in a few minutes. Prince Fyne was loading his camera and accidently swallowed a roll of film … and Prince Dandi's watching him to see what develops.

King (*rising disgustedly*) Doh. I don't believe you know where *any* of them are. (*To Ambrose*) Lord Chamberlain … throw this person out of the Castle and find the princes at once.

Ambrose (*glancing off* R *in relief*) No need, Sire. Here they come *now*.

The fanfare sounds again as the three princes enter, all richly dressed

The King sits again. As the Courtiers and Guests defer to the princes, they approach the throne and kneel

King (*impatiently*) Oh, never mind the formalities. Stand up. Stand up.

They do so

(*Eagerly*) Who's got the Golden Net?

Peerless *None* of us, Father. But we all know *what* it is.

King (*impatiently*) Well, of course we do. I told you that yesterday. What *I* want to know is *where* it is?

Peerless It's all around us. The Golden Net that can encompass the world, yet be drawn through a wedding ring is Love.

King (*blankly*) Love?

Courtiers and Guests look at each other in bewilderment

But that's *ridiculous*. (*He rises*) I don't believe it.

Fyne Well, that's what they *told* us.

King That's what *who* told you?

Peerless The old woman in the forest, and the mysterious girl who lives with her.

Fyne and Dandi nod their agreement

King (*dejectedly*) Then ... there isn't a *real* Golden Net at all? And I can't give up the throne? (*He sits in despair*)
Dandi (*disappointedly*) Doesn't look like it.
Ambrose (*hastily*) You could always set them *another* task, Your Majesty.
Peter (*helpfully*) Course you can. There must be hundreds of things you can choose from. How about... (*He names an improbable topical task*)
King (*brightening*) Yes. That *is* an idea. But it'll have to be something more difficult than *that*. Now let me see... (*He plunges into thought*)
Peerless Then while you're thinking about it, Father, I'd like to return to the forest and claim my future bride.

Everyone reacts in surprise

King (*startled*) Future bride? (*Flustered*) Who *is* she?
Peerless I've no idea ... but she's the most beautiful girl I've ever seen and I'll never be happy again unless she agrees to marry me.
King (*reeling*) Oh, my goodness. You'd better tell me all about her.
Peerless I will. If I can only find the words.

No. 8 Song (Peerless and the Others)

After the song there is a loud wailing off R

As everyone reacts, Dame Lovelorn hurries in, wearing another eye-popping creation

Dame Ohhhhhh. Help. Help. Somebody help. (*She staggers dramatically*)

Peerless quickly supports her

Peter (*recognizing her*) It's the old woman from the forest.
King (*standing indignantly*) How *dare* you burst into my Royal Castle? Who *are* you?
Dame (*weepily*) Dame Lovelorn, Your Majesty. But you can call me Hernia.
King (*blinking*) Really? And what do you want ... er ... Hernia?
Dame (*sniffling*) I want your support. That nasty old witch, Queen Venoma's kidnapped my beautiful Princess Rosamund, and I can't find her anywhere.
Peerless (*startled*) You mean the girl in your garden was a *princess*?
King But that's the girl... (*He realizes*) Oh, no. (*He sits heavily*)
Peerless (*anxiously*) What is it?
King She's the one Queen Venoma wants to marry Prince Ghastly.

Dame That's right. (*She sniffles*)

Peerless (*aghast*) But she *can't*. She's going to marry *me*.

Peter Not if you can't find her, she's not.

Peerless (*defiantly*) Then in that case, I'll search the world for her. She'll marry Prince Ghastly over my dead body.

King (*horrified*) But if *you* go off looking for her, we'll have to wait till you're back before I can send you on another quest. You could be gone for *years*, and *I'll* have to stay on the throne. (*In a flash of inspiration*) Just a minute. Wait. Wait... I've got it. (*He chortles*) It's the very thing. I'll give you each six months ... and whoever returns with the most beautiful bride will be given the crown.

Fyne (*brightening*) Oh, well... He's not going to find his princess in *that* time, so you might as well give it to me now. *My* girfriend's gorgeous. She's got cheeks like rosy apples, lips like cherries, skin like a peach's...

Dandi That's not a girlfriend. It's a fruit salad. (*Scornfully*) You haven't a chance of winning. (*Proudly*) *My* girlfriend's not only beautiful, she never answers back.

Fyne No. She's frightened to open her mouth in case somebody sticks an apple in it.

Fyne and Dandi prepare to fight

King (*hastily*) Boys, boys, boys. Now that's *enough*. I will not have disturbances in Castle Splendid.

There is a terrific crash of thunder and the Lights flicker madly

As everyone cowers, Queen Venoma enters DL *in a green follow spot. She is in a fury*

Venoma Where is she? What have you done with her? Return her to me at once.

King (*terrified*) I don't know what you're talking about. Return who?

Venoma (*savagely*) Don't play the innocent with me.
Within the forest deep we sped, my fingers round her wrist.
No chance escape within her grasp; unable to resist.
Yet even as the bound'ries of my gloomy Realm were neared,
I stumbled, lost my grip, and lo ... the princess *disappeared*.

Peerless (*delightedly*) You mean ... you've lost her?

Venoma (*laughing balefully*) Oh, no. Out of sight, maybe, but certainly not lost. (*Fiercely*) Where else would she return to but the side of that stupid old crone who hid her for so long? (*She glares at the Dame*) Now produce her this instant or *suffer the consequences*.

Mother Goose enters R, *followed by Ghiselle*

Mother Goose (*cheerfully*) Temper, temper, Venoma.
       This time you're out of luck.
       They don't know where the Princess is.
Venoma (*contemptuously*)   Well, well. It's Mother *Duck*.
Mother Goose (*smiling*) You'll never find young Rosamund, for with *my* magic spells
       I whisked her off to where, in peace and safety, she now dwells.
       Despite your pow'rs, she's out of reach, so cease this foolish quest.
       If you persist, I promise you, Prince Peerless, here, will come off best.
Venoma (*balefully*) You overestimate your skills. My magic is equal to yours. (*Scornfully*) And as for Prince Peerless... (*She laughs*) He couldn't say boo to a goose.
Mother Goose (*chiding*) A rather silly statement... and I'm sure it isn't true.
       But here's a goose who's not afraid to say a boo to *you*. (*She gives a signal to Ghiselle*)

Ghiselle shakes her feathers, scrapes her foot on the floor, then, lowering her head, charges at Venoma

Venoma gives a shriek of fear and rapidly exits L, *followed by Ghiselle*

The green follow spot goes out. Everyone looks relieved

King (*weakly*) Oh, thank goodness you arrived in time.
Dame *And* saved my little princess. I can't wait to see her again.
Peerless Me neither. (*Eagerly*) Where is she?
Mother Goose (*shaking her head*) Alas, not even you must find her hiding place just yet.
       Queen Venoma may well return, it's best not to forget.
       But never fear. When danger's past, I'll bring her to your side,
       And then with joyous bells a-ring, you'll claim your lovely bride.

Mother Goose exits R

Peerless (*hurrying* R *after her, calling*) But how soon will *that* be? (*He halts helplessly*) She's gone. (*He turns back*) And we don't even know how *long* we'll have to wait. (*Dismayed*) It could be *years*.
Dame Oh, no.

Fyne and Dandi exchange hasty looks

Fyne (*gleefully*) That's fine by *us*. The longer *she's* hidden away, the better chance *we've* got of winning the crown.

Dandi (*agreeing*) That's right. If she's not back in six months' time, one of *us'll* be the new King. (*He smirks at Fyne*)

Ambrose (*shocked*) But that's not fair. We'll call the whole thing off till the poor girl turns up.

King (*indignantly*) We certainly *won't*. I don't want to be King for ever ... and besides... I've already given my word. (*To Peerless*) I'm sorry, Peerless, but you'll just have to hope that she comes back in time.

Peerless (*protesting*) But I can't stay here and do *nothing*, Father. I don't care about the crown, but I've got to find Rosamund and make sure she's all right.

Peter (*alarmed*) But you *mustn't*. You heard what Mother Goose said. And what about Queen Venoma?

Peerless With any luck our paths'll never cross ... but if they do ... well ... she'll soon find out I'm no pushover. Now enough of the protests. It's time to begin the search for the missing Princess.

No. 9 Song (Peerless and the Others)

At the end of the song, Peerless moves UC *and the Principals and Chorus form a tableau as they wave him farewell. The Lights fade rapidly and——*

—the CURTAIN *falls*

ACT II

Scene 1

The Forest of Mysteria

Full set. A clearing by a waterfall in an ancient forest. Gnarled trees conceal entrances L and R, and dappled sunlight illuminates the scene

As the CURTAIN *rises, Gypsies in colourful costumes are singing and dancing in the clearing. Esmeralda, the Gypsy leader, sits on a log DL, watching*

No. 10 Song (Gypsies)

At the end of the song, Bluemalkin appears UR and moves LC

As she does so, all the Gypsies defer to her. She is an elderly cat in a high-necked, flowing gown, trimmed with fur. Over this is a top coat with bell sleeves, and also trimmed with fur. From the back of this, a soft, bushy tail curls up towards her shoulders. On her head is a matching soft, furry hat to which is attached a long chiffon scarf that wraps loosely around her neck. In her left paw she grasps her rod of office, which is topped with a crowned cat. A small pouch of gold is held in her right paw. As she arrives LC, the Gypsies stand

Bluemalkin (*kindly*) Once more, dear friends, I welcome you all to Mysteria and the Kingdom of the White Cat. (*To Esmeralda*) But tell me, Esmeralda... What news of Prince Peerless and his search for Princess Rosamund?

Esmeralda The same as before, my Lady Bluemalkin. With every passing day, his heart grows heavier, yet his search goes on without rest.

Bluemalkin And the witch, Queen Venoma?

Esmeralda (*amused*) Still casting her spells and vowing revenge ... but no nearer to finding the Princess than Peerless himself.

Bluemalkin (*sighing gently*) Then nothing has changed, it seems, and time grows shorter. (*She hands her the gold purse*) But take this gold for your assistance, and as you depart our enchanted Kingdom, our thanks go with you.

The Gypsies defer again as Bluemalkin turns and moves upstage to exit R

Esmeralda opens the pouch and looks inside as the other Gypsies crowd around her

Esmeralda (*delightedly*) Enough for all. Tonight, my friends, we shall feast in style. A thousand blessings on her feline Majesty, the White Cat.

The Gypsies cheer, and a reprise of their song and dance is performed before they exit R *in a very cheerful mood*

Peerless enters UL. *His clothes are travel-worn and dusty and a fardel tied to a stick rests on his shoulder*

Peerless (*wearily*) Almost six months of searching, and still no trace of her. (*He yawns*) I'm so tired. And what's worse, I've absolutely no idea where I am. Just lost in yet another great forest and not a soul in sight. (*He yawns again*) It's no use. I can't go any further. I'll have to rest. (*He glances* DR) Perhaps I can curl up beneath that tree? (*He crosses wearily to the tree* DR *and sinks to the ground. Eyes closing*) Just a few minutes and I'll be on my way again. She must be somewhere... (*He sinks into sleep*)

The Lights dim and Queen Venoma appears DL *in a green follow spot*

Venoma   (*gazing at him balefully*) Alas, young Prince, your search now
                     ends.
                For here, away from all your friends
                And interfering Mother Goose,
                On *you*, my magic powers I'll loose.
                Your toes within this soil will root;
                Your fingers lengthen, branch and shoot.
                And cloaked in green you'll ever be...
                No more than just a forest *tree*. (*She laughs*)

As Queen Venoma moves to approach the sleeping Peerless, a triumphant expression on her face, Bluemalkin enters R

Venoma halts in surprise

Bluemalkin (*firmly*) If this young prince you mean to harm, think twice
                     before you try.
                Our law decrees, whilst in this realm, his guardian am I.
Venoma And who are *you*, if I might be so bold as to ask?
Bluemalkin The Lady Bluemalkin, protector of all pure-hearted humans who venture to this secret place.

Venoma (*scornfully*) And am *I* to fear the mewlings of a talking *cat*? (*Harshly*) Begone ... lest I draw your teeth and claws.

Bluemalkin (*firmly*) This mewling cat, I think you'll find, has naught to fear from you.

By power of my magic stave, I bid you, ma'am, adieu. (*She points her cat-staff at Venoma*)

The green light surrounding Venoma at once turns white and she screeches with pain and staggers back

Venoma (*writhing*) Stop. Enough. I yield. I yield.

Bluemalkin advances on Venoma

Venoma retreats further, then turns and staggers off

Bluemalkin lowers her staff and the white light vanishes

Bluemalkin As homeward bound the Witch Queen limps for many weary hours,

She'll rue the day she mocked me and the White Cat's mighty powers.

But now, there's work that must be done; a journey we must make, (*She moves to Peerless and prods him with her staff*)

So leave your dreams, young sleeping prince. It's time that you awake.

Peerless (*sleepily*) What? (*He sees her and sits up*) A cat. In human clothes and carrying a staff. I must be dreaming. (*He rubs his eyes*)

Bluemalkin (*kindly*) Arise, Prince Peerless. The White Cat knows for what you seek, and bids me guide you to her wond'rous Palace.

Peerless (*scrambling to his feet; bewildered*) I don't understand. You know my name... And who on earth's the White Cat?

Bluemalkin Queen of Mysteria and the only one who can help you find the Princess Rosamund and achieve your heart's desire. Now come. (*She extends a paw to him*)

Peerless But how did she know I was here?

Bluemalkin The White Cat knows *everything*, for as she dreams, all is revealed to her.

Peerless I'd no idea cats *did* dream.

Bluemalkin Oh, yes. We all have our dreams.

No. 11 Optional Song (Bluemalkin)

At the end of the song, Bluemalkin exits DR, *followed by Peerless, his stick and fardel forgotten*

Dandi and Fyne enter furtively UL. *Dandi moves in a sideways crab-like motion as they move* R

Dandi (*hissing*) This way. This way. (*He beckons to Fyne*)

Fyne (*halting*) Wait a minute. Wait a minute. You've been walking like that for miles now. What's wrong with you?

Dandi It's that new medicine the doctor gave me. It's got side effects.

Fyne slaps Dandi's shoulder in exasperation

Owwww. What was *that* for? (*He rubs his shoulder*)

Fyne (*annoyed*) It's no wonder we can't keep up with that sneaky brother of ours if *you're* going to mess about. Just let him find this missing princess and we're *never* going to get the crown. He's got to be stopped.

Dandi (*sulkily*) What for? *I* won't get it anyway. *My* girlfriend's gone off with another feller.

Fyne (*curiously*) What for?

Dandi Because I took her to the Isle of Wight on the Royal yacht last week, and as soon as they recognized me, all you could hear was mooing.

Fyne Mooing? You mean *booing*, you fathead.

Dandi No, I don't. It was Cowes week.

Fyne slaps Dandi's shoulder again

Fyne (*tartly*) You're not the *only* one who's lost his girlfriend, you know. I got rid of mine *yesterday*. Talk about turning *nasty*. I bought her a real silk scarf and when she unwrapped it, she said "Oh, I don't believe it. How on earth can a beautiful scarf like this come from such a common little worm?" Well … I didn't expect *gratitude*, but there was no need to get *personal*.

Dandi So if neither of us has a girlfriend any more, Peerless's *got* to win.

Fyne No, he hasn't. We just have to make sure he never finds this Princess Rosamund, then head straight back to Euphoria and put my brilliant plan into action.

Dandi (*puzzled*) Which plan's that?

Fyne (*smugly*) Never you mind. But it'll make quite sure *he* won't get a look in. (*Delightedly*) Oooh, I can't wait for that Coronation. (*Dreamily*) Just think of it. King Fyne the Frivolous. (*Happily*) Smashing.

Dandi And what about me?

Fyne Well, it's obvious, isn't it? You'll be King Dandi the Daft.

Dandi What are you talking about? We can't both be King.

Fyne Oh, yes, we can. We're going to rule Euphoria together.

No. 12 Song (Fyne and Dandi)

At the end of the song, Fyne and Dandi hurry off R

Peter enters UL, *dressed as a Cub Scout. He is followed by Dame Lovelorn, who wears the uniform of a Brownie*

Peter (*cheerily*) Hiya, kids.

Audience response

Dame (*hissing at him*) Shhhhhhhh.
Peter (*surprised*) What? What?
Dame (*heavily*) We're supposed to be following Prince Peerless without him knowing about it, aren't we? How can we do it quietly if *you're* screaming your lungs out all over the place?
Peter (*soothingly*) OK, you don't have to worry, Hernia. With all these trees around, he won't hear a thing. Besides ... we've been walking all day and it's time we had a rest. Let's sit on this log over here. (*He indicates the log*)
Dame Good idea.

They move to the log and sit

Ooooh. That's better. But we mustn't stay too long. After all... (*Coyly*) We don't want folks getting the wrong idea, do we? You and me. All alone in the middle of this romantic forest. (*She simpers*)
Peter (*uneasily*) It's certainly quiet, isn't it?
Dame (*glancing around*) Yes. Reminds me of the place where I met my fifth husband.
Peter (*startled*) Fifth husband? How many have you had?
Dame Four. (*She chortles and pushes him playfully*)
Peter (*alarmed*) Here. I hope you're not thinking *I'm* going to marry you?
Dame 'Course not. We'll let the vicar do it. (*She puckers her lips at him*)
Peter (*protesting*) But I *can't* marry *you*. I'm not well. I keep having funny turns. Only last week I thought I'd turned into a *bridge*.
Dame (*surprised*) Oh, I say. Whatever came over you?
Peter Half a dozen cars, buses, lorries...

A large orange drops off the tree above him and hits him on the head

Owwww. (*He rubs his head*) What was that?
Dame (*looking at it*) Looks like an *orange*.
Peter Don't be daft. There's no orange trees in *this* country.
Dame I know. But... (*She realizes*) Here ... just a minute. (*She looks up*) There *could* be. There could be. We might be sitting under the famous Tree of Truth.

Peter Tree of Truth? (*He glances upwards*)
Dame (*excitedly*) Yes. Yes. I read about it in the *Sunday Sport*. If anybody
  sits under the Tree of Truth and tells a lie, an orange falls down and hits 'em
  on the head.
Peter (*scornfully*) Give over. And even if there *was* a Tree of Truth, it
  wouldn't drop an orange on *me*.
Dame Why *not*?
Peter Because I don't *tell* lies.

An orange falls and hits him on the head

  Owww. (*He rubs his head again*)
Dame (*chortling*) You see? You see? You told a lie.
Peter (*indignantly*) No, I *didn't*.

Another orange falls on his head

  Owww. (*He glares at the tree*) I've never told a lie in my life.

Another orange falls and hits him. He falls backwards on the log

  Owwwww. (*Scrambling up*) There must be a pigeon up there *knocking*
  'em down. Let's change places.

Dame edges over and Peter sits in her old position

  That's better. (*Warily*) We'll talk about something else, shall we?
Dame (*shrugging*) All right, then. (*Coyly*) Er ... do you think I'm prettier
  than Madonna [or other famous name]?
Peter Prettier than Madonna? You?
Dame Yes.

Peter turns aside and laughs then sobers and turns back

Peter Oh, yes. Yes. I do. I do.

*An orange falls and hits him on the head. He falls backwards off the log again,
scrambles up and regains his place*

Dame (*not noticing*) And ... er ... can you smell anything *unusual*?
Peter Unusual? (*He sniffs cautiously and grimaces*) Oh, *yes*. One of us must
  have trodden in something. (*He quickly checks his shoes*)

Dame (*simpering*) Silly. (*She pushes him playfully*) It's my new perfume. Moonlight in Manchester. They make it out of chip fat and Boddington's.
Peter Oh, yes. I thought I recognized it. It's my favourite scent.

An orange falls and hits him, knocking him off the log again

Dame (*not noticing*) Oh, go on. (*She simpers*) I know you don't mean that.
Peter (*re-seating himself*) Of course I mean…

He looks up to see an orange slowly descending on an invisible nylon thread

(*Hastily*) I mean… I *should* have said… I've never smelt anything *like* it.

The orange rises again and vanishes from sight

Dame (*happily*) So you do think it suits me?
Peter (*relieved*) Oh … it's definitely…

The orange appears again

(*Seeing it*) …*different*.

The orange rises and vanishes

Dame (*frowning*) How do you mean, different?
Peter (*at a loss*) Well … it's…

The orange appears

(*Seeing it*) …quite *strong*.

The orange rises

Dame (*surprised*) Strong? But it's supposed to be a *feint* perfume.
Peter (*aside*) Yes … one whiff of it and everybody faints. (*To her*) No, no. What I'm *trying* to say is … it's exactly the sort of perfume a woman like you *should* be wearing.
Dame (*pleased*) So does it drive you wild with passion?
Peter Well … er … er… (*He looks up into the tree*)
Dame (*ecstatically*) Ooooooh. Quick, quick. Give me a kiss. (*She grabs hold of him*)
Peter (*recoiling*) What for? What for?
Dame Because I've never kissed a man before. (*She puckers her lips at him*)

Peter Neither have I.

Dozens of oranges crash down on top of them and they fall off the log

Black-out

Scene 2

Outside the White Cat's Palace

A lane scene. The backdrop depicts the glittering exterior of the White Cat's fantastic Palace. It is evening

Cats in colourful and distinctive military uniforms enter to perform a tap dance routine

No. 13 Dance (Cats)

At the end of the dance, all exit L

Mother Goose and Ghiselle enter R

Mother Goose By rights, I should be rather cross. I thought I'd made it clear,
Prince Peerless stayed where he was safe whilst *I* would deal with matters here. (*She sighs*)
But those in love act foolishly and laugh in danger's face. (*She wags her finger at the audience*)
Don't smile and shake your heads. It's true of all the human race.
(*Thoughtfully*) So what to do? I must confess it was my firm intention
To outwit evil Venoma *without* The White Cat's intervention.
Now, with Peerless palace-bound to learn where Rosamund's concealed,
The danger is, Queen Venoma will learn it too and *never* yield.
Ah, well … the story's not yet told. There's more adventure still,
Ere Prince and Princess meet again … for better or for ill.

With a wave of her wooden spoon, Mother Goose exits R, *followed by Ghiselle*

Bluemalkin enters L, *followed by Prince Peerless*

Bluemalkin (*halting and indicating*) Welcome to the Palace of Her Majesty, the White Cat.

Peerless (*crossing her and gazing at it in wonder*) It's absolutely amazing. Like nothing I've ever seen before. (*He turns to face her*) And you're sure she can tell me where Rosamund is?

Bluemalkin Within those enchanted walls lies the answer to all you wish to know. Farewell ... and good fortune be with you. (*She prepares to exit* L)

Peerless (*anxiously*) But aren't you coming in with me?

Bluemalkin (*shaking her head*) My task is done, but there's nothing to fear. The White Cat herself will be there to greet you.

Bluemalkin exits L

Peerless (*to himself*) Is this the end of my search, then? Will the White Cat *really* help me to find Rosamund? (*Brightly*) Well ... I'm not going to learn anything by standing out here ... but if I *do* find her, Queen Venoma had better watch out, for I don't intend to lose my future bride a second time.

No. 14 Song (Peerless)

At the end of the song, Peerless exits R

The Lights fade down fast

Scene 3

Inside the White Cat's Palace

A great hall, a breathtaking room of absolute splendour with a small flight of wide stairs leading up to a balustraded platform that runs the full width of the set. A huge window dominates the backdrop, through which can be seen a starry and moonlit sky. Ornate gold and marble pillars mask entrances and exits L *and* R. *Huge candelabra provide the lighting*

When the scene begins, a stately gavotte is taking place, performed by cats in elegant suits and gowns

Suddenly the tinkling music ceases, and an extremely brassy piece of music replaces it as a very "modern' cat (Tigger-toes) appears at the top of the stairs

The dancers move L *and* R *as he/she vamps its way down the stairs and launches into a raucous jazz dance or song into which the others may join if required. At the end of the song/dance, the soloist exits up the staircase to a short reprise and the original dancers move into their original positions to conclude their own routine with the tinkling gavotte*

No. 15 Dance and Song/Dance (Cat Courtiers and Tigger-toes)

At the end of the dance, they freeze in position

Peerless (*off* R) Hallo? Is anybody there?

At once, the Courtiers exit L *and* UR

Peerless cautiously enters DR *and gazes around in awe*

Hallo?

The Lights fade to a total Black-out and UV lighting is brought into play. Only Peerless can now be seen. Soft music begins to play on pan pipes or flute

What's happening?

Two pairs of white hands float through the air supporting an "invisible" table (see Author's Notes). This is placed slightly above Peerless, and the hands vanish. As they do so, two more pairs of hands enter, appearing to have something stretched between them. The hands hover over the table, then suddenly a tablecloth appears which is laid over the invisible table. The hands vanish. Another pair of hands floats on, supporting a chair. This is placed R *of the table and the hands indicate for Peerless to be seated. As he does so, the hands signal and another pair of hands floats on with a napkin which they then tie around the Prince's neck. A knife and fork appear, followed by a white dinner plate. A series of covered salvers float on, supported by white hands. The salvers are placed on the table and the covers removed to reveal various edible dishes such as chicken, boar's head, bowls of peas, carrots, sweetcorn, etc. A large bowl of fruit is carried on, a wine goblet appears, and is placed next to Peerless. The hands vanish. Peerless meanwhile begins to mime eating and drinking. A large and brightly coloured moth enters and hovers around the table. Now and again, Peerless brushes it away, but the moth keeps returning. A pair of hands appear and catch the moth before exiting with it. Peerless sits back from the table. At once, an army of hands appears and everything is quickly cleared. As Peerless rises, the chair is whipped from behind him and vanishes into the wings. He is left alone in the darkness. The UV is switched off, the music ceases, and the Lights slowly rise again*

The White Cat stands C *at the top of the stairs. She is dressed in a high-necked, pure white gown of silk edged with thick white fur. Behind her, a luxurious white tail hangs. A diamond encrusted silver crown is on her head and a white feathered fan is held in one paw. The more spectacular her appearance, the better*

White Cat (*kindly*) Greetings, Prince Peerless, and welcome to my Royal Court.

She descends the staircase regally and as she does so, Peerless drops to one knee

(*Amusedly*) No need for such formality. Despite my wealth and title, I am nothing more than a cat.
Peerless (*gallantly*) But the loveliest I've ever seen.
White Cat Indeed? (*Coyly*) Then would you forget the girl you seek and choose *me* for your future bride? (*Amused*) I think not. (*She flutters her fan*)
Peerless (*rising eagerly*) Do you know where she is, Your Majesty? Where Mother Goose has hidden her?
White Cat I know she is safe and I know she is well, but until Queen Venoma gives up her search, I am forbidden to reveal her whereabouts.
Peerless (*taken aback*) Then … you can't help me, after all. And not only have I lost Rosamund, but the crown of Euphoria as well.
White Cat (*gently*) If a crown is all you wish, I invite you to share *mine*. In this Kingdom of eternal bliss are wonders such as humans have never seen.
Peerless (*sadly*) I thank you, Your Majesty. But without her, a crown means nothing. I thank you for your hospitality, but with your permission, I must leave the palace to continue my search. (*He bows and turns to exit*)
White Cat (*suddenly*) Wait.

He stops and turns back

Perhaps there *is* a way to help you. (*She holds out her paw to him*) Come. Let us walk in the garden while I think.

Peerless takes the White Cat's paw and they exit L

The Lights lower to half

Fyne and Dandi furtively enter DR

Dandi (*gazing around in awe*) So this is [local night spot or Council offices].
Fyne (*pushing him*) Fathead. (*He glances round*) I wonder where we really are?

Dandi Well, it's definitely not a National Trust place.

Fyne How do you know that?

Dandi There was nobody at the door taking money off you.

Fyne (*pushing him again*) Idiot. Now listen. If you ask me, there's nobody here at all and a place like this must have plenty of empty rooms. Right?

Dandi Right.

Fyne So the minute we find Peerless, we grab him, lock him inside one of 'em, then get back to Euphoria straight away and put my secret plan into action.

Dandi Smashing. (*Puzzled*) But you still haven't told me what it is.

Fyne Oh, all right, I'll tell you *now*. But… (*He glances off* R *and reacts*) Look out. Somebody's coming.

They attempt to hide behind each other

Peter enters DR

Peter Hiya, kids. (*He sees the princes and reacts with surprise*) What are *you* two doing here? (*Suspiciously*) You're not following Prince Peerless, are you?

Fyne (*defensively*) What if we are? He's our brother.

Dandi (*indignantly*) Yes. And we only want to make sure nothing happens to him.

Peter OK. Well, you don't have to worry about *that* because it's just what *we're* doing as well. Me and Dame Lovelorn.

The brothers look at each other in dismay

Mind you. I don't know where she's got to. You haven't seen her, have you?

The Dame enters DR *in another outrageous outfit*

Dame (*beaming*) Here I am, dear. Sorry I'm late, but I've been talking to one of the ducks on the pond.

Peter (*startled*) Eh?

Dame Oh, they all talk round here, you know. Animals, birds, fish. If it lives round this place, it'll talk to you.

Fyne (*looking askance at her*) So … what were you saying to it then? This duck.

Dame Well… I asked him why he had a *brown* beak and all the others had *yellow* ones.

Dandi (*curious*) And what did he say?

Dame Well ... he said he could *fly* as fast as all the others, but he couldn't stop as quick. (*She glances round*) Oh, I say. Look at this floor. It's covered in cat hairs. I bet the folks who live here haven't swept up in months.

Peter (*scornfully*) Swept up? We're living in modern times now, Hernia. Not the Dark Ages. They wouldn't sweep up in a place like this. They'd have vacuum cleaners.

Dame (*huffily*) Don't talk to *me* about vacuum cleaners. I tried to order one on the internet last month and they told me they'd send it by post the following day.

Fyne And didn't it come?

Dame It never got the chance. I told 'em to keep it. Who'd be daft enough to expect a vacuum cleaner through the post? They'd never get it though the letterbox.

Dandi (*uneasily*) Well, I don't know about you three, but *I'm* not sure I like this place. It's a bit on the creepy side.

Peter (*looking around*) You're right. It wouldn't surprise me if it was *haunted*.

Dame (*scornfully*) Don't be daft. There's no such thing as ghosts.

Fyne Oh, yes, there is. I met one last year and asked how much it would charge me to give Dandi a scare on Halloween Night.

Peter And what did it say?

Fyne It said for ten pounds, it'd scare him out of his wits... (*He gives a ghostly moan*) So I gave it five.

Dame Five?

Fyne Yes. Dandi's only a halfwit. (*He chortles*)

Dandi Go on. Go on. Point the skinger of fawn. But if I get frightened to death, I'll never speak to any of you again.

Peter Oh, don't worry. I know a way of making sure *nobody* gets scared. All we have to do is sing a little song ... and if anything nasty and creepy comes along, it'll frighten it away.

Dame Are you sure?

Peter 'Course I am. Now what are we going to sing?

Fyne How about "Daddy wouldn't buy me a bow-wow"? We all know that.

Dame Good idea. And while we're singing it, the boys and girls can keep an eye out for any ghosts and things, and warn us if one comes along. (*To the audience*) Will you do that for us?

Audience response

Peter Off we go then.

They begin to sing

A Ghost passes L *to* R *behind them and exits again*

As the audience reacts, the singers stop in confusion

Fyne What is it? What's wrong?
Peter They say they've just seen a ghost.

Everyone quickly looks around

Dame (*frowning*) Well, I can't see anything.
Dandi Neither can I.
Peter (*realizing*) Oh, they must be pulling our legs. They haven't seen anything at all. Let's carry on singing.

They sing again

> *The Ghost enters* R, *crosses behind them and exits* L

As the audience reacts, the singers halt again

Fyne What are they shouting for now?
Dandi (*nervously*) They say it's just been back again.
Peter Well, where did it go?
Dame Perhaps we'd better have a look round. (*She indicates* L) Go that way.

To the accompaniment of "creepy" music, they tiptoe cautiously round in a large circle, peering and glancing

> *As the last one passes the wing* L, *the Ghost emerges and follows the line round. As the leader arrives back in his/her original position* DS, *the Ghost exits* R

Fyne Well, I didn't see any ghost. They're having us on.
Dandi Yes. But they're still shouting. I think we should have a look the other way.
Peter All right then. Back the other way.

They re-trace their steps clockwise

> *Again the Ghost tags on to the end of the line and exits* R

Dame (*disgustedly*) There's nothing there at all.
Fyne They're having us on.
Dandi Let's carry on singing and ignore 'em.

They sing again

The Ghost creeps out and stands behind them, waving its arms gently

The singers falter again as the audience reaction grows

Peter *(to the audience)* What's wrong now? *(He reacts to the response)* Oooer. They say it's behind us.
Dame Oh, no, it isn't.

Audience response

All Oh, no, it isn't.

Audience response

Peter Well, I'll tell you what we'll do. We'll all count to three, then we'll turn round and grab it. Are you ready?

They count to three. As they do so, the Ghost sinks downwards and when they turn, they look over it, then turn to face front again, disgustedly, saying "Nothing there at all", "Take no notice in future", "Rotten things, scaring us like that", etc. They start to sing again. The Ghost rises and taps Fyne on the shoulder

Fyne turns, sees it, screams and rushes off, chased by the Ghost

Someone notices Fyne is missing and halts the others. After general ad-libbing, the singing re-commences

The Ghost enters and taps Dandi's shoulder. He turns, sees it, screams and dashes off, chased by the Ghost

Peter notices Dandi has gone and halts the Dame. After further ad-libbing, the pair start singing again

The Ghost enters and taps Peter's shoulder. Peter turns and sees it, screams and runs off

The Dame halts

Dame *(scared)* Ooo-er. They've all gone now. I'm on me own ... by meself and nobody's with me. I'd better sing a bit louder. Just a minute. I'm so scared I've forgotten what we were singing. I'd better find out. *(To the Pianist)* Excuse me, Mr Pianist, but what is it you're playing?

Pianist (*calling loudly*) It's a piano, you silly old sausage.

Dame Oh, yes. (*She chuckles weakly*) Thank you. (*She clears her throat and starts to sing again in a tremulous voice*)

The Ghost enters, taps her on the shoulder and she turns to it. The Ghost screams and runs off

The Dame looks baffled, then follows it, shaking her head

The Lights become brighter and Peerless and the White Cat enter L

Peerless I don't understand. How can returning home help me to find Rosamund?

White Cat Just do as I say and happiness will be yours. Despite Queen Venoma's threats, the Princess *shall* become your bride. I, the White Cat promise it.

Peerless But when will I see her again?

White Cat Sooner than you think. In the throne room of your father's castle, I'll reveal her hiding place myself.

Peerless (*surprised*) You mean ... you're coming with me?

White Cat What else can I do? Your joy will be my joy and that of the Princess, too.

Peerless (*delightedly*) Oh, thank you, Your Majesty. You've made me the happiest man on earth.

No. 16 Song (Prince and White Cat)

As the song continues, the Cat Courtiers may enter and join in

At the end of the song, there is a tableau finish with Peerless and the White Cat on the stairs and the scene ends with a snap Black-out

SCENE 4

On the way back to Euphoria

A lane scene. This can be the same as Scene 2 if required. Daylight

Queen Venoma enters L *in a green spotlight. She clutches what appears to be a raven or rook to her breast, and a triumphant smile is on her face*

Venoma At last. At last. My search for the missing princess is almost over.

(*She laughs*) Little did the White Cat realize, that with the aid of my magic crystal, every word she spoke was heard by *me*. When she appears with Rosamund at the castle of King Pat-a-cake, my darling son will also be there … ready to claim his bride. I must summon him at once. (*She faces the exit* L) Fly, little bird. Wing your way to Despondia and summon Prince Ghastly to my side. (*She tosses the bird upwards and into the wings*) Fly, my precious one. Fly.

Venoma cackles with laughter and exits L, *the green spotlight also vanishing*

Mother Goose and Ghiselle enter R

Mother Goose (*concerned*) Oh, dear. Exactly what I feared. The cat's out of the bag.
　　　　Or will be soon, which means, of course, a vict'ry for that ancient hag.
　　　　(*Firmly*) There *must* be something I can do to undermine her plan.
　　　　If not, it seems poor Rosamund may *have* to wed that ugly man.
　　　　His awful features, sad to say, cause everyone to mock.
　　　　No wonder, when a glance from him could stop the Town Hall clock.

Ghiselle nudges her gently and Mother Goose stoops for Ghiselle to whisper in her ear

　　　　What's that? You've had a sudden thought?
　　　　The answer's clear to see?
　　　　Do *what*? (*She listens again, then stands impressed*) Well, well. You're right, of course.
　　　　(*She chuckles*) You've got more brains than *me*.
　　　　(*To the audience*) We must away. There's work to do. Ghiselle and I intend
　　　　To bring at last this merry tale, to satisfact'ry end.

Mother Goose brandishes her spoon gaily and exits R, *followed by Ghiselle*

Ambrose totters on L, *followed by an anxious King Pat-a-cake*

King Can you see them, Ambrose? Is anybody there?
Ambrose (*peering off* R) Not a sign, Your Majesty. And the six months is up tomorrow.

King (*relieved*) Oh, thank goodness for that. If none of them get back in time, I won't have to give the throne up, will I?

Ambrose (*startled*) But … but I thought you *did* want to give it up, Sire.

King (*embarrassed*) So did I. But since they've been away I've realized I *like* being King, after all. And if one of them *does* come back with a beautiful bride… I won't be King any longer. (*Fretting*) We've got to think of something, Ambrose. How can I make sure that I don't have to lose the crown? (*He thinks furiously*)

Ambrose (*shocked*) But you gave your word, Sire.

King (*testily*) I know. I know. But what's the use of being a king if you can't change your mind? (*Brightening*) Aha … I have it. We're miles away from the castle now, so if *I* return to it with a bride more beautiful than anyone else's … I don't have to give the crown to anyone, do I? (*He beams*)

Ambrose (*shocked*) But that's cheating. And besides … you can't get *married*, Your Majesty.

King (*indignantly*) Why not? It's thirty years since the Queen and crew were lost in that terrible storm that sank the Royal Yacht. And if I hadn't been cast away on a desert island, *I* could have been lost, too.

Ambrose (*nodding*) That's true. You were missing for six whole years before you managed to *escape* from it. Though you never told us how, did you?

King (*airily*) Oh, there was nothing to it. Luckily, a brand new lifeboat drifted by and I managed to drag it on to the beach, knock it to bits and build a raft. (*Firmly*) Now stop wasting time, Ambrose. We've got to get back to Euphoria and find me a new wife.

Ambrose (*woefully*) Can't we have a sit down first, Your Majesty? I don't think I can walk ten miles right now.

King (*sternly*) Don't be a *wuss*, Ambrose. Besides … there are two of us, aren't there, so it'll be only five miles each. Now come along. Left, right. Left, right.

The King exits L briskly, followed by a weary Ambrose

Peter enters R, followed by Dame Lovelorn in yet another creation

Wearily, Peter crosses L without speaking

Dame (*surprised*) Just a minute.

Peter halts and looks at her without interest

Aren't you going to say "Hiya, kids"? (*She indicates the audience*)

Peter Oh. (*To the audience, indifferently*) Hiya, kids. (*He begins to walk again*)

Dame (*to him*) What's *wrong* with you?

Peter (*miserably*) What do you think's wrong? We've lost all *three* of the princes now, so there's nothing to do but go home again.

Dame Ooooh, don't be so *miserable*. I'm not. One of 'em's bound to find out where Rosamund is … and even if they don't, Mother Goose'll look after her till old Venoma's cleared off. (*Coyly*) Anyway … while we're waiting for 'em to turn up again, we could be getting to know each other a bit better. I mean … you don't want to marry a *stranger*, do you?

Peter I don't want to marry *anybody*.

Dame (*playfully*) Of course you *do*. And you're exactly the kind of feller *I'm* looking for. You're breathing.

Peter (*protesting*) But I *can't* marry you. Hernia. You're *years* older than I am.

Dame Well… I shouldn't let *that* worry you. There's many a good tune played on an old fiddle, you know.

Peter Yes … but not when it's riddled with wood-worm. Besides … you've been married before, haven't you?

Dame Of course I have, but not for very long. I lost 'em all in accidents. (*She sniffles*) My *first* and *second* husbands died from eating poisoned mushrooms, and my *third* husband fell over a cliff and broke his neck.

Peter How did that happen?

Dame He didn't like mushrooms. (*Passionately*) Oh, come on … propose to me. There might be some snow on the roof, but there's plenty of flames in the fireplace.

No. 17 Song (Dame and Peter)

At the end of the song, the Lights rapidly fade down

SCENE 5

The Great Throne Room Again

As Act I, Scene 5. Daylight

King Pat-a-cake sits on his throne, watching the Court Dancers. Courtiers and Guests are grouped around the perimeters

No. 18 Dance (Court Dancers)

At the end of the dance, all applaud as the dancers exit

Ambrose hurriedly enters UR *and approaches the throne*

Courtiers and Guests chatter silently and ignore the following dialogue

Ambrose (*breathlessly*) Your Majesty. Your Majesty.

King (*rising eagerly*) What is it, Ambrose? Have you found me a bride?

Ambrose Too late, Sire. There's a silver coach approaching the castle gates, and Prince Peerless is riding beside it. He must have found the Princess.

King (*despondently*) Oh, no. I just *knew* this was going to happen. A few more hours and there'd have been nothing to worry about, but now I'm *bound* to lose the crown. (*He sits heavily*) You'd better announce them, Ambrose.

Ambrose moves R *and bangs his rod of office on the floor to attract the attention of the Courtiers, etc.*

Ambrose (*announcing*) His Royal Highness, Prince Peerless and The Princess Rosamund.

A fanfare sounds as Peerless enters RC, *accompanied by the White Cat. Peerless is dressed finely, as befits him, and wears a scabbard and sword. The White Cat wears a floor-length and enveloping hooded cloak of white, trimmed with white gossamer-like fur. A fur-trimmed white muff hangs on a cord around her neck. All that is visible of her to the audience is her face. As the Courtiers and Guests defer to them, the pair approach the throne and defer to the King*

King (*unhappily*) All right. All right. There's no need to bow. You're the only one to arrive back with a bride ... so you may as well take the crown now. (*He takes it off*) But at least let me see what she looks like.

Peerless (*rising*) No, no, Father ... this isn't...

Before he can say more, the White Cat rises and slips back the hood to reveal her cat's head and ears. Everyone reacts with loud gasps, etc.

King (*gaping at her*) A cat? (*He rises*) You want to marry a cat?

Everyone begins to titter and point derisively

Peerless (*embarrassedly addressing everyone*) You don't understand. This is *the White Cat*.

King (*sniggering*) We can see *that*. Would she like a saucer of milk? (*He laughs*)

Ambrose (*giggling*) Or a tin of Kit-e-kat? (*He falls about with laughter*)

*Everyone laughs loudly, saying "Here, puss, puss, puss", "Meow. Meow",
etc.*

Peerless (*in distress; calling over the noise*) Be quiet. Stop laughing... She
wants to tell us where Rosamund's hidden.
King Oooooooh. It's a talking cat. (*He shrieks with laughter*)

Everyone doubles up, shrieking with laughter

*The White Cat looks distressed, then pulls the hood over her head again
and hurries off* UL

Hastily, Peerless follows

*The laughing King sits again, mopping at his eyes, and the noise gradually
lessens*

(*Replacing his crown*) That's the funniest thing I've ever heard. My
youngest son ... in love with a cat. (*He chuckles*)
Ambrose (*sobering*) That's all very well, Your Majesty ... but if the other
two princes don't return today, you've no choice but to give him the crown.
You said it yourself and everyone heard. Whoever produces the most
beautiful bride will be the next King. No-one said it couldn't be a cat.
King (*realizing*) You're right. (*He rises hastily*) Quick. Quick. Find me a
bride at once. Anyone will do. She *has* to be more beautiful than a mangy
old cat.

Dame Lovelorn and Peter enter DR

Peter Hiya, kids.

Audience response

King (*seeing the Dame*) Aha, the very person. (*He hurries down to her*)
Hernia... Hernia *beloved*... (*He kneels in front of her*) Marry me.

Courtiers and Guests react

Dame (*startled*) Eh?
King Say you'll be mine, and I'll love you forever.
Dame (*overcome*) Oooh, I say. (*To the audience*) Did you hear *that*, boys and
girls? He said he'd love me forever. (*She simpers, then sobers and turns*

back to him) Yes ... well, it's all right you saying that *now*, but what *I* want to know is would you *still* be saying it when I'm old and ugly?

King *(passionately)* Of course I would, my angel. You may grow *older*, but in my eyes you could never grow uglier.

Dame *(pleased)* Oooh, you saucy old thing. *(She sighs)* Well... I'm sorry, Pat-a-cake ... but I've already blighted me trough to somebody else, *(she takes Peter's arm)* and he'd be ever so upset if I changed me mind.

Peter shakes his head frantically in denial

Besides ... we're getting married this afternoon, so we'll be in China tonight on our honeymoon. *(She simpers)*

King *(rising)* Don't be ridiculous. You can't get to China today.

Dame Why not? It's not all that far. I phoned [local travel agency] to ask how long the flight'd take, and the woman there said "Just a minute, dear".

Ambrose looks off R and reacts in surprise

Ambrose Oh, my goodness... *(Hastily announcing)* His Royal Highness, Prince Fyne ... and a lady.

King *(groaning)* Oh, no.

The King totters L as a fanfare sounds

Fyne enters UR with Dandi, who is dressed as a bare-footed harem beauty in chiffon baggy trousers, jewelled bra, etc., long wig and a chiffon yashmak

Fyne *(importantly)* Make way for the future Queen ... Princess Jelibelli of Wallapaloo who will now perform for you the famous Dance of the Seven Veils.

As they move DC hand in hand, with Dandi mincing and fluttering, and the Courtiers and Guests deferring to them, vaguely eastern music begins to play and Dandi atttempts to perform a sensuous dance with laughable results

No. 19 Dance (Dandi)

King *(interupting suspiciously)* Just a minute. Just a minute.

The music stops

I recognize those Calvin Kleins. That's not a dancing girl. *(He crosses to Dandi and pulls off the wig and yashmak)* It's *Dandi*.

Everyone reacts

Dandi (*grimacing in mortification*) Does this mean we don't get the crown?
King (*indignantly*) It certainly *does*. (*He thrusts the wig and yashmak at Dandi*) How *dare* you try to trick me like this? (*Firmly*) Well, that's done it. As *none* of you have produced a beautiful bride, *nobody's* getting the crown. I'll keep it for myself. (*He turns away beaming happily*)

Mother Goose enters R

Mother Goose A moment, hasty Pat-a-cake. It may be time at last,
To keep the promise once I made and break the spell I cast.
The White Cat you so cruelly mocked, alone doth hold the key
To bring Prince Peerless happiness and set the Princess free.

The King and others look mortified

Come join us, faithful Peerless ... with White Cat by your side...
That should she wish it, once again you'll find your future bride. (*She waves her spoon*)

The crowd parts as Peerless enters UL, *escorting The White Cat, who, as before, wears the hooded cloak. The couple move* C

(*To them*) To you alone, White Cat, I gave the pow'r to break that spell.
Without your help, for evermore, in hiding must the Princess dwell.
Yet if you will, by dagger sharp, that long enchantment ends,
And Rosamund shall be once more restored to home and friends.
Peerless (*alarmed*) Dagger? What dagger?

The White Cat produces a small dagger from the muff around her neck and holds it high. As all react in horror, she stabs herself. There is a flash and an immediate Black-out with concerned cries from everyone. At once the Lights go up and Princess Rosamund is standing there, smiling. No trace of the White Cat remains. All react

(*Delightedly*) Rosamund. It was you all the time.

Rosamund and Peerless embrace

Dame (*overcome*) My little girl. (*She hurries to her and hugs her*)

King (*despairingly*) Well, that's it *again*. There can't be *anyone* more beautiful than her. Now I *have* to give up the throne.

Princess (*amused*) No need for that, Your Majesty. I have Seven Kingdoms of my own and I'm sure they'll be quite enough for Peerless and myself.

As the King beams happily at the news, Queen Venoma appears DL *in a green spotlight*

Venoma (*harshly*) I think not, my precious Princess.

Everyone but Mother Goose reacts and draws back

(*Moving towards Rosamund*) Now that I've found you again, you shall come with *me* to Despondia … and the bridal chamber of my darling son Prince Ghastly.

Princess (*defiantly*) Never.

The Dame clutches Rosamund to protect her

Peerless (*stepping forward and drawing his sword*) One more step and you'll have *me* to reckon with.

Venoma (*laughing*) Fool. Dolt. Idiot. Not even Mother Goose can defeat me now.

She points her finger at him and the sword drops from his hand. Everyone gasps

Peter (*anguished*) Somebody *do* something. Hernia … sing to her.

Ghiselle enters DR *… a large envelope in her beak. Ignoring everyone else, she waddles over to Venoma and pushes the envelope at her*

Venoma (*glowering*) What's this? (*She snatches it and looks at the writing on the envelope*) A letter from Prince Ghastly? (*She opens it and reads*) "Dear Mumsy-wumsy … for twenty years, while you've been using *your* magic to search for Princess Rosamund, I've stayed at home listening to folks make fun of my ugly face and crooked body. But since Mother Goose used *her* magic to make me the handsomest man in Despondia, the palace has been packed with beautiful girls all wanting to marry me. This being the case, I decided not to wait any longer for your return and have chosen one of them. The wedding's planned for today. *I've* taken over the Kingdom, and *you've* been banished. Love and kisses, Prince Ghastly."

(*She tosses the letter aside in a fury*) Banished? Banished? From my own kingdom? (*She screeches*) He can't do this. Just wait till I get my hands on him.

Venoma exits L, raging, and the green spotlight is extinguished

As everyone expresses relief, Mother Goose moves between the Prince and Princess

Mother Goose (*brightly*) Ring out the bells without delay
This happy pair shall wed today.
For once they're joined in wedded bliss,
And vows are sealed with tender kiss,
I'm sure that I can guarantee.
No more of Venoma they'll see.
From hence their lives shall fill with laughter,
And both live happily, ever after. (*She waves her wooden spoon gaily*)

As all cheer, music begins and the whole company, led by Peerless and Rosamund sing a celebratory song

No. 20 Song (Company)

At the end of the song, there is general celebration as the scene ends

SCENE 6

A Corridor in Castle Splendid

A lane scene. Song sheet as required

No. 21 Song

At the end of the song, the Lights rapidly fade

SCENE 7

The White Cat's Ballroom and Finale

A full set. The glittering ballroom of the Enchanted Palace of Cats. Full lighting

As bright music begins, Dancers in their cat costumes are performing a short routine. As the end of the routine nears, they exit L and R and the walkdown commences as follows:

> *Chorus of Singers*
> *Dancers*
> *Tigger-Toes*
> *Esmeralda*
> *Peglegasus*
> *Bluemalkin*
> *Ambrose*
> *Mother Goose and Ghiselle*
> *Queen Venoma*
> *King Pat-a-cake*
> *Prince Fyne*
> *Prince Dandi*
> *Peter Piper*
> *Dame Lovelorn*
> *Prince Peerless and Princess Rosamund*

When the line-up is completed, the music ends and Mother Goose steps forward

Mother Goose Our pantomime is over. The mummery is done.
>   We hope we've entertained you with our dances, songs and
>   fun.
>   And maybe in the years to come, you'll still remember that
>   You spent a pleasant evening once, in the company of…
All White Cat.

The entire company then sing a reprise of one of the brighter songs used during the show, and at the end of this——

—the Curtain *falls*

FURNITURE AND PROPERTY LIST

Further dressing may be added at the director's discretion

ACT I

Prologue

On stage: Frontcloth depicting **Mother Goose**'s arbour

Personal: **Mother Goose:** large wooden spoon (carried throughout)

Scene 1

On stage: Backdrop depicting ancient city square

Off stage: Mop and bucket (**Dame Lovelorn**)
Stout rope (**Peter**)

Personal: **King:** gold crown (worn throughout)
Queen Venoma: jewel-topped cane, black crown, rings on fingers
Dame Lovelorn: mob cap, apron, necklace of brightly coloured
beads
Prince Fyne: small crown
Prince Dandi: small crown
Prince Peerless: money pouch with bank notes (worn throughout)
Ambrose: large scroll

Scene 2

On stage: Backdrop depicting ancient forest

Off stage: Crystal ball (**Venoma**)

Scene 3

On stage: Garden backdrop
Small rustic bench

Off stage: Horseshoe (**Prince Peerless**)

Personal: **Queen Venoma:** small framed photograph

Scene 4

On stage: Backdrop depicting castle interior

Off stage: Large blackboard (**Ambrose**)

Personal: **King:** stick of chalk

Scene 5

On stage: Small dais. *On it*: great throne
              Candelabra
              Chandeliers

Off stage: Rod of office (**Ambrose**)

ACT II

Scene 1

On stage: Gnarled trees
              Log
              Oranges

Off stage: Fardel tied to a stick (**Prince Peerless**)

Personal: **Bluemalkin:** rod of office, small pouch of gold

Scene 2

On stage: Backdrop depicting **White Cat**'s Palace

Scene 3

On stage: Ornate gold and marble pillars
              Candelabra

Off stage: Table (**SM**)
              Tablecloth (**SM**)
              Chair (**SM**)
              Napkin (**SM**)
              Knife and fork (**SM**)
              White dinner plate (**SM**)
              Covered salvers with chicken, boar's head, bowls of peas, carrots,
                sweetcorn (**SM**)
              Large bowl of fruit (**SM**)
              Wine goblet (**SM**)
              Moth (**SM**)

Personal: **White Cat:** fan

Scene 4

On stage: Backdrop depicting lane scene

Off stage: Raven or rook (**Queen Venoma**)

Scene 5

On stage: Small dais. *On it*: great throne
              Candelabra
              Chandeliers

Off stage: Large envelope (**Ghiselle**)

Personal: **Prince Peerless:** scabbard, sword
              White Cat: small dagger

Scene 6

On stage: Backdrop depicting Castle Splendid

Scene 7

On stage: Ornate gold and marble pillars
              Candelabra

LIGHTING PLOT

Property fittings required: chandeliers, candelabra
Various interior and exterior settings

ACT I, PROLOGUE

To open: Early morning lighting, with light mist

Cue 1   **Mother Goose** and **Ghiselle** exit   (Page 2)
             Fade lights rapidly to black-out

ACT I, SCENE 1

To open: Bright, sunny lighting

Cue 2   The **King** ad-libs on his collection   (Page 4)
             Fade lights, bring up green follow spot on **Venoma**

Cue 3   **Venoma** exits   (Page 6)
             Fade out green follow spot, return lights to normal

Cue 4   **Peerless** exits   (Page 16)
             Fade lights to black-out

ACT I, SCENE 2

To open: Dappled lighting

Cue 5   **Mother Goose** and **Ghiselle** exit   (Page 17)
             Brighten lights slightly

Cue 6   **Peter** exits   (Page 20)
             Dim lights, bring up green follow spot on **Venoma**

Cue 7   **Venoma** exits   (Page 20)
             Rapidly fade lights

ACT I, SCENE 3

To open:	Overall general lighting	
Cue 8	**Rosamund** turns to exit	(Page 27)
	Dim lights, bring up green follow spot on **Venoma**	
Cue 9	**Venoma** and **Rosamund** exit	(Page 27)
	Fade out green follow spot, bring up overall lighting	
Cue 10	**Dame Lovelorn** exits	(Page 28)
	Black-out	

ACT I, SCENE 4

To open:	Overall general lighting	
Cue 11	The **King** and **Ambrose** exit	(Page 30)
	Fade lights rapidly	

ACT I, SCENE 5

To open:	Candelabra and chandeliers lighting	
Cue 12	**King**: "…disturbances in Castle Splendid."	(Page 34)
	Flicker lights madly	
Cue 13	**Queen Venoma** enters	(Page 34)
	Bring up green follow spot on **Venoma**	
Cue 14	**Venoma** and **Ghiselle** exit	(Page 35)
	Fade out green follow spot	
Cue 15	**Principals** and **Chorus** form a tableau	(Page 36)
	Fade lights rapidly	

ACT II, SCENE 1

To open:	Dappled sunlight	
Cue 16	**Peerless** sinks into sleep	(Page 38)
	Dim lights, bring up green follow spot on **Venoma**	

| *Cue* 17 | **Bluemalkin** points her cat-staff at **Venoma** | (Page 39) |
| | *Turn spot on* **Venoma** *to white* | |

| *Cue* 18 | **Bluemalkin** lowers her staff | (Page 39) |
| | *Cut white spot on* **Venoma** | |

| *Cue* 19 | **Peter** and **Dame Lovelorn** fall off the log | (Page 44) |
| | *Black-out* | |

ACT II, SCENE 2

To open: Evening lighting

| *Cue* 20 | **Peerless** exits | (Page 45) |
| | *Fade lights fast* | |

Act II, SCENE 3

To open: Overall lighting, starry moonlit sky through window

| *Cue* 21 | **Peerless**: "Hallo?" | (Page 46) |
| | *Fade lights to total black-out, bring up UV lighting* | |

| *Cue* 22 | **Peerless** is left alone in the darkness | (Page 46) |
| | *Cut UV lighting, slowly bring up overall lighting* | |

| *Cue* 23 | **Peerless** and **White Cat** exit | (Page 47) |
| | *Lower lights to half* | |

| *Cue* 24 | The **Dame** exits | (Page 52) |
| | *Brighten lighting* | |

| *Cue* 25 | At end of song | (Page 52) |
| | *Snap Black-out* | |

ACT II, SCENE 4

To open: Daylight lighting

| *Cue* 26 | **Queen Venoma** enters | (Page 52) |
| | *Bring up green spotlight on* **Venoma** | |

EFFECTS PLOT

ACT I

Cue 1   **King**: "…disturbances in Castle Splendid."   (Page 34)
           Terrific crash of thunder

ACT II

No cues